STO

5-2-73

COOKING WITH MUSHROOMS

VALERIE MARCH

Cooking with Mushrooms

DRAKE PUBLISHERS INC NEW YORK

ISBN 0–87749–435–5

LCCCN 72–10500

Published in 1973 by
Drake Publishers Inc
381 Park Avenue South
New York, N.Y. 10016

Printed in Great Britain

Contents

Introduction

IT IS OFTEN the occasion that dictates the recipe, so I have arranged the recipes in this book according to the occasion, although many of them will suit any meal or time of day. For instance, there's a chapter on freezer dishes but the recipes can be used even if you don't have a freezer.

A recipe is not a doctor's prescription but a guide to successful cooking; be ready to adapt a recipe to your personal requirements and use the ingredients available to you.

Where I have recommended a particular grade of mushroom, it is because it will, in my opinion, give the best result; but if you can't buy this grade in your area don't be put off the recipe; use whatever grade is available.

Mushrooms come in three grades, each referring to a stage of growth. The Button mushroom is a small closed one. As the mushroom begins to open and show a little of the delicate gills, it becomes a Cup mushroom. The fully ripe mushroom, the Open or Flat grade, has the most mature flavour.

Providing you buy good fresh specimens, mushrooms can be stored for a number of days in a domestic refrigerator or in a cool larder. To store, leave them in the supermarket pack, or leave them in the greengrocer's paper bag and put this into a plastic bag, or turn them from the shopping container into a sealed kitchen container. All these ways will prove successful.

Mushrooms are one of the few foods available to us that has little or no waste; we can eat the full weight that we buy. Rinse the caps of the mushrooms under a running tap and dry them on kitchen paper. There is no need to peel cultivated mushrooms.

A final note—many cooks spoil the delicate flavour and texture of mushrooms by cooking them too long so they become leathery. Test them from time to time with a fork.   V.M.

Make Now—Cook Later

THESE DISHES can all be prepared in advance by the busy housewife and then finished when ready to serve. Follow the recipe to the ● then leave the food in a cool place until you are ready to complete the dish.

Bacon Croquettes

For 4–6

10 oz cooked bacon (minced)	*3 tablespoons fresh bread-*
4 oz mushrooms (minced)	*crumbs*
1 oz green pepper (minced)	*¼ teaspoon thyme*
1 oz onion (minced)	*2 eggs*
2 oz cheese (grated)	*breadcrumbs*
	fat for frying

1. Mix all the minced ingredients together with the cheese.
2. Stir in the fresh breadcrumbs and season with salt, pepper and thyme.
3. Bind with beaten egg to a firm paste.
4. Shape into croquettes on a floured board; chill in the refrigerator.

●

5. Coat croquettes in egg and breadcrumbs and fry in hot fat until golden brown. Drain on kitchen paper. Serve with chutney.

Crab Cups

For 4

1 medium onion	*¾ oz flour*
½ lb mushrooms	*¼ pint double cream*
⅓ pint dry cider	*6 oz crabmeat*
1 bay leaf	*2 tablespoons dried bread-*
1 oz butter	*crumbs*

1. Slice onions and mushrooms.
2. Put the onion and mushrooms into a pan, pour in the cider, season with salt, pepper and bay leaf. Simmer for about 10 minutes.
3. Heat butter in a pan, add the flour and stir in the cider stock from the other pan. Bring to the boil.
4. Simmer for 3 minutes then blend in the cream and check seasoning.
5. Mix the mushrooms, onion and crabmeat with the sauce.
6. Divide the mixture between four individual overproof dishes.

•

7. Top each dish with breadcrumbs and bake in oven 400 degrees F, mark 6 for about 15 minutes.

Mackerel Shirlerie

For 4

4 mackerel	*1 lb tomatoes*
lemon juice	*½ lb mushrooms*
3–4 tablespoons oil	*¼ teaspoon thyme*

1. Fillet the mackerel and sprinkle with lemon juice.
2. Heat the oil in a frying pan and fry the fish for 1 minute on each side. Remove from the pan.

3. Skin and slice the tomatoes. Slice the mushrooms.
4. Put into the frying pan and season with thyme, salt and pepper.
5. Cook the vegetables until they become a thick pulp.
6. Spread on top of the fish and put into an ovenproof dish.
Cover with a lid or foil.

•

7. Bake in oven 350 degrees F, mark 4 for 30 minutes.

Mermaids' Delight

For 4

1¼ *lb white fish*   ½ *pint milk*
3½ *oz butter*   6 *oz Gruyère cheese (grated)*
1 *oz flour*   ¾ *lb mushrooms (sliced)*

1. Put the fish into a pan, add enough water or fish stock barely to cover the fish. Season with salt and pepper, cover and cook until fish flakes easily.
2. Melt 1½ oz butter in a pan, stir in the flour and add the milk. Season and bring to the boil.
3. Stir in the fish, flaked, and the cheese. Turn into individual ovenproof dishes.
4. Turn the mushrooms in hot butter, season with salt and pepper and cook for 3 minutes.
5. Top each dish with mushrooms. Cover with lids or foil.

•

6. Put the dishes into oven 375 degrees F, mark 5 for about 20 minutes or until well heated.

Ocean Pie

For 4

½ lb smoked haddock	3 oz prawns (peeled)
2 scallops	½ pint coating white sauce
¼ lb soft roes	2 tablespoons double cream
¼ lb button mushrooms	1½ lb creamed potatoes
	½ oz butter

1. Cut the haddock into 2-inch squares. Clean and slice the scallops.
2. Put the scallops and soft roes into an ovenproof dish. Season. Then add the haddock squares.
3. Slice the mushrooms; put mushrooms and prawns into the white sauce. Simmer gently for 3 minutes.
4. Remove from the heat and stir in the cream. Check seasoning.
5. Pour the sauce over the fish and top with well-beaten potato. Dot with butter.

•

6. Cook in oven 425 degrees F, mark 7 for about 25 minutes.

Cockney Pie

For 4

1 onion (sliced)	black pepper
½ lb mushrooms (sliced)	1 lb sliced boiled beef
2 oz butter	¾ lb cooked carrots (sliced)
1 oz flour	1 tablespoon demerara sugar
½ pint beef stock	
2 teaspoons wine vinegar	

1. Slice the onion and mushrooms. Heat the butter in a pan and gently cook the onion and mushrooms until tender.

2. Stir in the flour then add the stock and wine vinegar. Season with salt and freshly ground black pepper. Bring to the boil and simmer for 2 minutes.

3. Put the sliced meat into an ovenproof dish and pour over the sauce.

4. Cover the dish with sliced carrots.

•

5. Sprinkle the brown sugar over the carrots.

6. Bake in oven 350 degrees F, mark 4 for about 30 minutes.

Country Chicken Pie

For 4

1 large sandwich loaf	*1½ oz flour*
3 oz butter	*¾ pint milk*
½ lb mushrooms (sliced)	*1 tablespoon lemon juice*
1 onion (sliced)	*1 tablespoon chopped parsley*
6 rashers streaky bacon (cut in strips)	*¾ lb cooked chicken (cut in pieces)*

1. Cut the crust off one side of the loaf; remove all the crumb from inside (use this for breadcrumbs).

2. Butter the inside of the loaf.

3. Heat the butter in a pan, add the mushrooms, onion and bacon and cook until tender.

4. Stir in the flour, then add the milk; season with salt and pepper and bring to the boil.

5. Stir in the lemon juice and parsley. Check seasoning.

6. Add the chicken to the pan and stir well over a low heat for a minute or two.

•

7. Pour the chicken sauce into the bread case; replace the crust.

8. Bake in oven 350 degrees F, mark 4 for 30 minutes.

Parmesan Cutlets

For 4–8

8 lamb cutlets	1½ oz Parmesan cheese
1½ oz butter	(grated)
½ lb mushrooms	1 tablespoon minced onion

1. Fry the cutlets in hot butter to seal them on both sides. Do not cook them completely.
2. Mash or mince the mushrooms and mix with the cheese and onion.
3. Cover one side of each cutlet with the mixture, pressing it down firmly onto the meat.
4. Put into an ovenproof dish.

●

5. Bake in oven 400 degrees F, mark 6 for 20–25 minutes.

Pork Cutlet Casserole

For 4

1½ oz dripping	black pepper
4 pork cutlets	4 tomatoes
½ lb mushrooms (sliced)	1 tin condensed vegetable
1 onion (sliced)	soup

1. Heat the dripping in a pan and seal the cutlets on both sides. Put cutlets into an ovenproof dish.
2. Turn the mushrooms and onion in the remaining fat and put into the casserole. Season with salt and freshly ground black pepper.
3. Skin and slice the tomatoes. Add to the dish and pour in the tin of soup.

●

4. Cook in oven 375 degrees F, mark 5 for about 45 minutes or until the meat is tender.

Venetian Liver

For 4

1 lb liver	*1 teaspoon chopped parsley*
1 onion (finely chopped)	*4 oz mushrooms (sliced)*
2 oz dripping	*lemon juice*
1 teaspoon mixed herbs	*¼ pint stock*

1. Cut the liver into strips.
2. Heat the dripping in a pan and lightly fry the onion.
3. Add the liver to the pan and turn in the hot fat for 1 minute.
4. Put half the liver into an ovenproof dish; add half the onion also.
5. Sprinkle with mixed herbs, parsley and lemon juice. Cover with half the mushrooms.
6. Put the other half of the liver and onion into the dish and top with remaining mushrooms. Pour in the stock and cover the dish.

●

7. Cook in oven 375 degrees F, mark 5 for 45 minutes.

Stuffed Mushrooms

For 2–4

12 Cup mushrooms	*1 tablespoon chopped parsley*
1 medium onion	*4 tablespoons fresh white*
6 oz bacon	*breadcrumbs*
2 oz butter	*oil*
sage	

1. Remove the stalks from the mushrooms.
2. Mince the mushroom stalks, onion and bacon together.
3. Heat the butter in a pan, add the minced ingredients and cook for 2 minutes.
4. Stir in a pinch of sage, chopped parsley and fresh breadcrumbs. Sprinkle with salt and pepper.

5. Brush the caps of the mushrooms with oil. Place the mushrooms in an ovenproof dish.
6. Fill the gills of the mushrooms with the stuffing.

•

7. Bake in oven 375 degrees F, mark 5 for about 30 minutes.

Savoury Stuffed Pancakes

For 4

½ *pint pouring batter*	*1 lb cooked minced beef in*
fat for frying	*gravy (fresh or canned)*
1 oz butter	*1 15½ oz tin tomato soup*
6 oz mushrooms (sliced)	*3 oz cheese (grated)*

1. Fry four good-sized pancakes in hot fat.
2. Heat the butter in a pan, add the mushrooms, season with salt and pepper and cook for about 4 minutes.
3. Turn the minced beef into the pan and mix well.
4. Put the pancakes flat on a table or board. Divide the meat into four portions and put onto the pancakes. Roll them up.
5. Put into an ovenproof dish. Pour over the soup and sprinkle each pancake with cheese.

•

6. Bake in oven 375 degrees F, mark 5 for about 30 minutes.

Cabbage Parcels

For 4

1 cabbage	*3 tomatoes (skinned and*
4 oz long grain rice	*sliced)*
2 oz butter	*1 teaspoon Soy sauce*
½ *lb mushrooms (chopped)*	½ *teaspoon mixed herbs*
2 oz onion (chopped)	⅓ *pint tomato sauce*
	3 oz cheese (grated)

1. Separate the cabbage leaves. Blanch the leaves in boiling salted water. Cut out any tough stalks.
2. Boil the rice in salted water until tender, drain well.
3. Heat the butter in a pan, add mushrooms and onion, season with salt and pepper and cook until tender.
4. Add the tomatoes, Soy sauce and mixed herbs; cook over a low heat for 5 minutes.
5. Stir in the cooked rice. Check seasoning.
6. Spoon the mixture onto the centre of the cabbage leaves, roll up leaves firmly and put into an ovenproof dish. Pour over the tomato sauce and sprinkle with grated cheese.

•

7. Bake in oven 375 degrees F, mark 5 for 45 minutes.

Egg and Leek Envelopes

For 4

4 leeks	*1½ oz butter*
12 oz mushrooms	*pinch mixed herbs*
4 rashers bacon	*4 eggs*

1. Slice leeks into rings. Slice mushrooms. Cut bacon into strips.
2. Tear off four good sized pieces of cooking foil.
3. Heat the butter in a frying pan; turn the leeks in butter until tender and lightly browned. Drain and divide between the four sheets of foil. Sprinkle leeks with salt and pepper.
4. Put mushrooms, bacon and mixed herbs into the pan. Cook for 4 minutes. Put a quarter on each foil sheet.
5. Make a small hollow in the centre of the vegetables. Break an egg into each one. Seal the foil parcels and put onto a baking sheet.

•

6. Bake in oven, 350 degrees F, mark 4, for 15–20 minutes. Open the parcels at the table.

Baked Cheese Roll

For 4

8 oz suet pastry	*1 hard-boiled egg (chopped)*
6 oz mushrooms	*½ pint cheese sauce*
1 oz butter	*1 oz butter (melted)*
6 oz boiled bacon (chopped)	*2 oz cheese (grated)*

1. Roll out the pastry to an oblong shape.
2. Chop the mushrooms and toss in hot butter with a little salt for 2 minutes.
3. Mix the bacon, mushrooms and egg with enough cheese sauce to bind the mixture together.
4. Spread over the pastry leaving a 1-inch border.
5. Brush the border with water and roll up the pastry. Make a few slits in the top.
6. Place the roll on a floured baking sheet.

•

7. Brush the pastry with melted butter and scatter cheese over the top. Bake in oven 375 degrees F, mark 5 for about 40 minutes.

Champignons Florentine

For 4

1½ lb fresh spinach (or frozen)	*½ teaspoon mustard*
3 oz butter	*4 oz cheese (grated)*
¾ lb mushrooms	*½ pint coating white sauce*
4 eggs	

1. Cook the spinach in a little salted water until tender. Drain well and stir in 1 oz butter.

2. Line the bottom of four small buttered ovenproof dishes with the spinach.

3. Slice the mushrooms and cook them in hot butter for 4 minutes, adding plenty of salt and pepper during cooking.

4. Edge each dish with mushrooms.

5. Break an egg in the centre of the mushrooms.

6. Stir the mustard and half the cheese into the white sauce, then pour into the dishes

•

7. Scatter the rest of the cheese on top of each dish. Bake in oven 350 degrees F, mark 4 for about 20 minutes.

Florentine Ravioli

For 3–4

2 oz butter	1½ lb spinach
1 oz flour	1 14 oz tin Ravioli with
½ pint milk	tomato sauce
2 oz Gruyère cheese (grated)	1 tablespoon breadcrumbs
6 oz mushrooms (sliced)	

1. Melt 1 oz butter in a pan, stir in the flour and cook for 1 minute. Stir in milk and seasoning, return to the heat and cook, stirring continuously until thick and creamy. Stir in the cheese.

2. Heat the remaining butter in another pan, add mushrooms and season with salt and black pepper. Cook for 3 minutes.

3. Cook the spinach for 5 minutes in boiling salted water. Drain well and chop.

4. Place the spinach at the bottom of a casserole, add the mushrooms and cover with the Ravioli. Top the dish with a thick layer of cheese sauce. Sprinkle with breadcrumbs.

•

5. Place in the oven at 400 degrees F, mark 6 for 20 minutes.

Spanish Bake

For 4

½ *lb mushrooms*	*black pepper*
4–6 rashers bacon	*4 eggs*
4 tomatoes	*2 tablespoons cream*
2 oz butter	*Parmesan cheese (grated)*

1. Chop mushrooms, bacon and tomato; sauté in hot butter. Season.
2. Turn into four buttered individual ovenproof dishes.
3. Break an egg on top of each dish, pour over a little cream and sprinkle with cheese.

●

4. Bake in oven 375 degrees F, mark 5 until eggs are just set—about 15 minutes.

Baked Fresh Haddock

For 4

1 whole fresh haddock (about	*1 small green pepper*
1¾ *lb)*	⅛ *pint dry cider*
knob of butter	*1 lemon*
½ *lb open mushrooms*	
bay leaf	

1. Clean the fish and remove any scales.
2. Butter the centre of a large sheet of cooking foil.
3. Put the fish on the buttered foil, the mushrooms round the fish and a bay leaf and slice of green pepper on top of the fish.
4. Pour the cider and a squeeze of lemon juice over the ingredients.
5. Season well with salt and freshly ground black pepper.

6. Bring the sides of the foil to meet on top and seal the edges together so that there is a space between the foil and the fish. Seal the ends firmly.

•

7. Cook in oven 425 degrees F, mark 7 for about 25 minutes.
8. Put the fish onto a serving dish and decorate with cooked mushrooms and slices of pepper and lemon.
May be served hot or cold.

Gammon Rolls with Mushroom Sauce

For 4–8

1½ lb fresh spinach	*8 thin gammon rashers*
2 hard-boiled eggs	*1 oz onion (grated)*
1 oz almonds (chopped)	*1½ oz flour*
3 oz butter	*¾ pint milk*
½ lb mushrooms	*parsley (chopped)*

1. Cook the spinach in a little boiling salted water. When tender, drain well and chop with a knife.
2. Chop the hard-boiled eggs and mix these, the almonds and ½ oz butter with the spinach.
3. Slice the mushrooms, toss in 1 oz hot butter, season with salt and pepper and cook for 3 minutes.
4. Mix half the mushrooms with the spinach.
5. Divide the spinach mixture into 8 equal portions, spread on the gammon rashers, roll up and secure with a wooden cocktail stick.
6. Prepare the sauce—heat the remaining butter in a pan and add the onion. Cook for 1 minute then stir in the flour.
7. Gradually add the milk, then the mushrooms and a little salt and pepper.

•

8. Grill the gammon rolls until tender and cooked through. Remove the sticks.
9. Bring the sauce to the boil and cook for 2 minutes.
10. Put the gammon rolls onto a hot dish, pour over the sauce and garnish with chopped parsley.

Meals Around the Clock

THIS SECTION contains dishes which are suitable at almost any hour; whether for breakfast, high tea, light lunch or a late snack. They are easily prepared and a number of them make use of convenience foods.

Grilled Mushrooms

Open mushrooms are the most suitable.

For 1 lb mushrooms allow 2 oz butter.

1. Remove the grid from the grill pan. Heat the grill.
2. Trim the mushroom stalks level with the edges of the caps.
3. Melt the butter in the grill pan. Dip the mushroom caps in the butter and put them, cap uppermost, into the grill pan. Grill for 2 minutes.
4. Turn the mushrooms, sprinkle the gills with salt and pepper and return the pan to the grill for a further 2–3 minutes.
5. Serve on hot buttered toast, as part of a mixed grill, or as a garnish or accompaniment to other dishes.

Fried Mushrooms

Small buttons or large open mushrooms are the most suitable.

For 1 lb mushrooms allow 2 oz butter.

1. Heat the butter, or part of the butter depending on the size of

the frying pan. Put the mushrooms into the pan, stalks upper-most.

2. Season well with salt and pepper; sprinkle with a little lemon juice.* Cover the pan with a well-fitting lid or cooking foil.

3. Cook over a moderate heat for 4–5 minutes. Do not turn the mushrooms over so that the juice remains in the mushrooms.

4. Serve on hot buttered toast or as part of a 'Mixed Fry' or as a garnish or accompaniment to many other foods.

* A variety of different herbs or sauces may be used to season the mushrooms during frying, as well as lemon juice.

Curried Mushrooms

For 4

2 medium onions (sliced)	½ pint fresh tomato pulp
3 tablespoons oil	1 lb mushrooms
2 teaspoons curry powder	½ pint stock

1. Fry the onions in oil until tender and light golden in colour.

2. Stir in the curry powder and tomato pulp; cook for 2 minutes.

3. Add 1 teaspoon salt, freshly ground black pepper and mush-rooms, cut into quarters if large.

4. Pour in enough stock to coat the mushrooms with sauce. Simmer for 20 minutes stirring occasionally.

5. Serve with long grain rice and mango chutney.

Soya Mushroom Savoury

For 4

2 oz butter	black pepper
1 lb mushrooms (sliced)	2 tablespoons double cream
2 oz split almonds	parsley (chopped)
1 tablespoon Soy sauce	hot buttered toast or
2 teaspoons Angostura	vol-au-vent cases
Bitters	

1. Heat the butter in a pan and turn the mushrooms and almonds in the butter.
2. Sprinkle with Soy sauce and Angostura Bitters, season with salt and freshly ground black pepper.
3. Cook over a fierce heat for about 3 minutes when most of the liquid will have evaporated.
4. Remove from the heat and stir in 2 tablespoons double cream and sprinkle with chopped parsley.
5. Serve on rounds of hot buttered toast or in vol-au-vent cases.

Devilled Mushrooms

For 4

3 oz butter
2 oz onion (finely chopped)
1 lb mushrooms (sliced)
*$\frac{1}{4}$ pint dry cider
*$\frac{1}{4}$ pint wine vinegar
*1 teaspoon Worcestershire
 sauce

*1 teaspoon mustard
*$\frac{1}{4}$ teaspoon Cayenne pepper
4–6 slices toast
1 lemon

1. Heat the butter in a pan and gently fry the onion.
2. Add the sliced mushrooms and turn over a fierce heat for 1 minute. Sprinkle with 1 teaspoon flour.
3. Stir in the starred ingredients; when well mixed, cover and simmer for 10 minutes.
4. Using a draining spoon, put the mushrooms into a hot dish.
5. Reduce the sauce by half over a fierce heat then pour into the dish.
6. Arrange triangles of toast round the edge and lemon wedges in the centre.

Bacon Snacks

For 4

6 slices white bread	1½ oz butter
shallow fat for frying	12 bacon rashers
12 cup mushrooms	chutney

1. Cut 12 circles, 2-inch diameter, from the slices of bread with a pastry cutter. Fry these in hot shallow fat until golden. Drain on kitchen paper and keep hot.
2. Fry the mushrooms in hot butter for about 4 minutes.
3. Stretch the bacon rashers with a round-bladed knife. Spread each rasher with a little chutney.
4. Wrap a bacon rasher round each mushroom and secure with a wooden cocktail stick.
5. Grill the bacon, turning the rolls frequently until evenly cooked. Remove the sticks.
6. Serve on the circles of hot bread with a green salad.

Crumpet Savoury

For 2–4

4 crumpets	6 oz mushrooms (sliced)
2 oz butter	1 oz flour
4 slices luncheon meat	⅓ pint milk
1 tablespoon onion (chopped)	3 oz cheese (grated)

1. Toast the crumpets. Butter one side, put onto an ovenproof dish and keep warm.
2. Heat the rest of the butter and fry the meat on both sides until golden brown. Place on top of the crumpets.
3. Fry the onion and mushrooms in the pan. Sprinkle with flour and gradually add the milk.
4. Bring the sauce to the boil, stirring all the time. Season well with salt and pepper.

5. Pour the sauce over the crumpets. Scatter cheese over the top and brown under a hot grill.

Minute Miser

For 4

*1 large tin meat balls in
  sauce*
½ lb mushrooms
1 oz butter
pinch mixed herbs

1 packet curled vermicelli
*1 tablespoon parsley
  (chopped)*
1 tablespoon chives (chopped)

1. Turn the meat balls into a pan and heat gently.
2. Slice the mushrooms and cook in hot butter, seasoned with mixed herbs, salt and pepper; simmer for about 4 minutes.
3. Cook the vermicelli as instructed on the packet. Drain well and arrange on a hot serving dish. Put the meat balls in the centre, cover with mushrooms, parsley and chives.

Brighter Beefburgers

For 4

8 beefburgers
oil for frying
6 oz mushrooms (diced)
6 oz cheese (grated)
½ teaspoon mustard

*1 tablespoon pickled beetroot
  (diced)*
*1 dessertspoon gherkins
  (diced)*

1. Fry the beefburgers in hot oil. Remove from the pan.
2. Turn the mushrooms into the oil, season with salt and pepper and cook until all the liquid has evaporated.
3. Allow the pan to cool, then mix all the other ingredients with the mushrooms.
4. Top each beefburger with a little of the mixture and finish under a hot grill.

Beefburger Sandwiches

For 4

1 lettuce
5 tablespoons oil
8 beefburgers

1 onion (sliced)
4 large open mushrooms
2 tomatoes

1. Clean the lettuce and arrange the whole leaves on a serving dish.
2. Heat some oil and fry the beefburgers on both sides. Drain on kitchen paper and keep hot.
3. Fry the onion until lightly browned; then the mushrooms for about 4 minutes. Season with salt and pepper.
4. Place 4 beefburgers on the lettuce leaves and cover them with onion; place another beefburger on the top and a whole mushroom on top of each. Garnish with sliced raw tomatoes.

Napolitan Hamburgers

For 4

4 slices bread
4 hamburgers
4 large flat mushrooms
melted butter

1 14 oz tin Spaghetti
Napolitan
3 oz Cheddar cheese (grated)

1. Cut circles out of the bread the size of the hamburgers. Toast the circles.
2. Grill the hamburgers and mushrooms, brushed with melted butter.
3. Heat the Spaghetti Napolitan.
4. Place the rounds of toast on a hot heatproof serving dish. Put a hamburger on each, topped with a mushroom; then pile the spaghetti on top and sprinkle with grated cheese.
5. Brown the cheese under a hot grill and serve at once.

Hawaiian Grill

For 4

4 tomatoes
½ lb open mushrooms
2 oz butter (melted)
8 chipolata sausages

8 pineapple rings
1 oz demerara sugar
watercress

1. Brush the halved tomatoes and mushrooms with melted butter. Season with salt and pepper.
2. Grill the tomatoes, mushrooms and sausages.
3. Brush one side of each pineapple ring with butter and sprinkle with brown sugar. Brown under the grill. Repeat on the second side.
4. Put a sausage through the hole in each pineapple ring and arrange on a hot dish. Set the tomatoes and mushrooms round the edge and garnish with sprigs of watercress.

Haricot Cream

For 4

2½ oz butter
½ lb mushrooms (sliced)
1 tablespoon onion (chopped)
1 oz flour
½ pint milk

black pepper
1 large tin Haricot beans
1 lb sausages (beef or pork)
4 rashers bacon
1 tablespoon chives (chopped)

1. Melt the butter in a pan, add the mushrooms and onion and cook until tender.
2. Stir in the flour and then the milk and bring to the boil. Season well with salt and freshly ground black pepper.
3. Drain the liquid from the tin of beans and stir the beans into the sauce.
4. In the meantime, grill the sausages and bacon.
5. Turn the Haricot cream into a hot dish and arrange the sausage and bacon on the top.
6. Garnish with chopped chives.

Frankfurter Sweetcorn

For 4

¾ *lb mushrooms*	*juice of ½ lemon*
1 small clove garlic	*1 large tin sweetcorn*
2 oz butter	*1 lb frankfurter sausages*
black pepper	*watercress*

1. Slice the mushrooms. Crush the garlic.
2. Heat the butter in a pan. Add the mushrooms and garlic. Season with salt, freshly ground black pepper and lemon juice. Cook over a moderate heat for 4–5 minutes.
3. Turn the sweetcorn into the pan and stir over a moderate heat until piping hot.
4. In another pan, put the frankfurter sausages into hot water and simmer gently until well heated.
5. Turn the mushrooms and corn onto a hot dish. Arrange the sausages on top and garnish with sprigs of watercress.

Savoury Stuffed Green Peppers

For 4

4 large green peppers	*3 tablespoons oil*
2 14 oz tins Ravioli	*4 oz cheese (grated)*
12 oz mushrooms (sliced)	

1. Put peppers onto a long fork in turn and hold over a hot burner on the cooker. When the skin is black all over, put into cold water and scrape with a knife. Cut off the top of the peppers and remove the centre and seeds.
2. Turn the mushrooms in hot oil, season with salt and black pepper. Cook for 3 minutes.
3. Put the mushrooms into the bottom of an ovenproof dish. Drain the sauce from the Ravioli over the mushrooms.
4. Fill the peppers with the Ravioli cushions and stand them on the mushroom base. Sprinkle cheese over the tops of the peppers.
5. Bake in oven 350 degrees F, mark 4 for about 30 minutes.

Aubergine Slice

For 4

dripping	*½ lb mushrooms (sliced)*
½ lb minced veal	*10 oz shortcrust pastry*
1 tablespoon onion (minced)	*1 tablespoon tomato paste*
black pepper	*2 tablespoons stock*
1 aubergine (diced)	*milk or beaten egg*

1. Heat 1 oz dripping in a frying pan, add the veal and onion; season with salt and freshly ground black pepper. Cook over a low heat for 5 minutes. Remove from the pan.
2. Add more dripping if required and turn the aubergine in hot dripping until well browned and tender. Remove from the pan.
3. Put the mushrooms into the pan, season with salt and cook for 3 minutes.
4. Line an 8-inch shallow ovenproof dish with half the pastry.
5. Turn all the fried ingredients into the pastry case.
6. Put the tomato paste into the frying pan, add the stock and cook together for a moment. Pour over the filling.
7. Cover the filling with the rest of the pastry. Make a decorative finish to the edges of the pastry. Brush with milk or beaten egg.
8. Bake in oven 400 degrees F, mark 6 for about 45 minutes.
9. Cut into slices and serve hot or cold.

Cornish Pasties

For 4

6 oz mushrooms (sliced)	*½ lb potatoes (peeled and sliced)*
4 oz onion (sliced)	
1½ oz butter	*½ lb chuck steak (diced)*
10 oz shortcrust pastry	*mixed herbs*
	beaten egg

1. Turn the mushrooms and onion in hot butter for 2 minutes.
2. Cut the pastry into four even-sized pieces. Roll each piece to a round shape and trim round a tea-plate.
3. Put a layer of potato across the centre of each pastry circle.
4. Cover with a layer of finely diced meat.
5. Then add the mushrooms and onion.
6. Sprinkle with salt, pepper and a pinch of mixed herbs.
7. Brush the pastry edges with beaten egg and bring the edges to meet on top of the filling. Press the pastry firmly together to keep in the steam.
8. Brush the outside of the pastry with egg and bake in oven 400 degrees F, mark 6 for 30 minutes; reduce the oven temperature to 350 degrees F, mark 4 and cook for a further 30 minutes.
9. Serve hot or cold.

Italian Medley

For 4

8–12 oz spaghetti	*½ teaspoon marjoram*
1 tablespoon oil	*1½ oz butter*
1 dessertspoon tomato paste	*12 oz mushrooms (sliced)*
1 large tin tomatoes	*4 large eggs*
1 teaspoon demerara sugar	

1. Cook the spaghetti in boiling salted water until tender; drain well.
2. Heat the oil in a pan, add the tomato paste and then the tin of tomatoes. Stir in the sugar and marjoram, season with salt and pepper. Cook over a moderate heat until the sauce begins to thicken.
3. Heat the butter in another pan. Add the mushrooms, season with salt and pepper and cook for 3 minutes.
4. Remove the mushrooms from the pan and fry the eggs in hot butter.
5. Turn the spaghetti onto individual hot plates. Put the mushrooms in the centre of each portion. Pour over the sauce and top each dish with a fried egg.

Egg and Mushroom Noodle Bake

For 4

8 oz noodles	1 teaspoon Soy sauce
3 oz butter	few drops Tabasco sauce
3 oz onion (sliced)	1 teaspoon mustard
½ lb mushrooms (sliced)	¾ pint milk
1½ oz flour	4 eggs
1 teaspoon Worcestershire	3 oz cheese (grated)
sauce	1 tablespoon breadcrumbs

1. Cook the noodles according to the packet instructions.
2. Heat 1 oz butter in a pan and cook onion and mushrooms for 4 minutes. Season well with salt and pepper. Put aside.
3. Heat the rest of the butter in the pan, stir in the flour, sauces and mustard.
4. Add the milk and bring to the boil. Check seasoning.
5. Mix noodles, onion and mushrooms into the sauce and turn into a greased ovenproof dish.
6. Make four wells in the mixture and break an egg into each.
7. Scatter cheese and breadcrumbs over the surface and bake in oven 400 degrees F, mark 6 for about 15 minutes.

Mushroom Scrambled Eggs

For 4

½ lb mushrooms	3 tablespoons top of the milk
1½ oz butter	4–8 slices hot buttered toast
8 eggs	

1. Slice the mushrooms. Turn them in hot butter, season well with salt and pepper and cook until the liquid has evaporated.
2. Break the eggs into the pan. Add the milk and stir with a wooden spoon over a low heat. Check seasoning.
3. When eggs are creamy, spoon over the hot toast and serve at once.

Egg and Mushroom Vol-au-Vents

For 4

2 oz butter
½ lb mushrooms (sliced)
1 oz flour
½ pint milk
onion salt

black pepper
4 large eggs
4 large vol-au-vent cases
(baked)

1. Heat the butter in a pan and cook the mushrooms for 3 minutes.
2. Stir in the flour; gradually add the milk. Season with onion salt and freshly ground black pepper. Stir well and bring to the boil.
3. Put the eggs into boiling water and cook for 4 minutes. Carefully remove the shells as the yolks will still be soft.
4. Have ready the hot vol-au-vents, place an egg in each and fill the case with mushroom sauce.

Egg and Caper Rolls

For 4

4 crusty rolls
6 hard-boiled eggs
1 tablespoon capers
½ pint white sauce

4 large open mushrooms
1 oz butter
parsley (chopped)

1. Cut the top off each roll and remove the crumbs from the middle of the roll.
2. Put the rolls into a cool oven to warm through.
3. Cut the eggs into quarters.
4. Put the eggs and capers into the white sauce. Check seasoning.
5. Grill the mushrooms in butter.
6. Fill the rolls with the egg and caper sauce.

7. Place a grilled mushroom on top of each roll.
8. Sprinkle with chopped parsley.

A substantial dish for a teenage party.

Anchovy Eggs

For 4

8 large cup mushrooms
1½ oz butter
2 oz anchovy fillets
  (about 16)

8 standard eggs
4–8 slices hot buttered toast

1. Grill the mushrooms in melted butter for about 5 minutes. Season well with salt and pepper.
2. Put the anchovy fillets in the grill pan and warm them under the grill.
3. Poach the eggs in boiling water.
4. Put the mushrooms onto a hot serving dish; put a poached egg on each mushroom and decorate the top with anchovy fillets.
5. Edge the dish with triangles of hot buttered toast.

Autumn Eggs

For 4

8 eggs
3 tablespoons oil
8 oz onions (sliced)
8 oz mushrooms (sliced)
1 lb tomatoes (skinned, sliced)

½ teaspoon sage
¼ pint dry cider
4 tablespoons peas (cooked)
4 tablespoons carrots (diced, cooked)

1. Cook the eggs in boiling water for 10 minutes.
2. Heat the oil in a frying pan, add onions, cook until tender.

3. Put mushrooms and tomatoes into the pan. Season with salt, pepper and sage. Cook until the liquid has evaporated.
4. Stir in the cider, peas and carrots. Simmer for 5 minutes.
5. Shell the eggs, put into a hot serving dish and pour over the sauce.

Simon's Savoury

For 4

6 thin slices white bread	*6 oz mushrooms*
3 oz cream cheese	*4 eggs*
1 small onion	*½ pint milk*
6 oz bacon	*½ teaspoon mixed herbs*

1. Spread one side of the bread with cream cheese.
2. Line a buttered ovenproof dish with the bread, cheese facing inwards.
3. Mince the onion, bacon and mushrooms.
4. Beat the eggs and milk with salt, pepper and mixed herbs. Stir in the minced ingredients.
5. Turn into the prepared dish.
6. Bake in oven 350 degrees F, mark 4 for about 45 minutes or until the mixture is set.
7. Garnish with chopped parsley.

Mushroom Omelette

For 1

1¼ oz butter	*1 teaspoon onion (chopped)*
3–4 oz mushrooms (sliced)	*2 eggs*

1. Heat ½ oz butter in a frying pan. Fry the mushrooms and onion, seasoned with salt and pepper, until tender and lightly browned.

2. Put a small knob of butter into an omelette pan, when hot, pour in the lightly beaten eggs, seasoned with salt and pepper.

3. Stir in the rest of the butter and the mushrooms. Cook over a fierce heat, shaking the pan occasionally to cook the mixture evenly.

4. Fold and turn the omelette onto a hot plate and eat at once.

Golden Omelette

For 2

1 oz butter	*4 eggs*
4 oz mushrooms (sliced)	*2 tablespoons cream*
1 small clove garlic (crushed)	*1 tablespoon thin strips red*
2 tomatoes (skinned and	*pimento (tinned)*
sliced)	*2 oz cheese (grated)*

1. Heat 1 oz butter in a frying pan. Add the mushrooms, garlic and sliced tomato. Season well and cook gently for 5 minutes.

2. Lightly beat the eggs and cream with salt and pepper.

3. Turn the eggs into a large hot buttered omelette pan; cook over a fierce heat, shaking the pan occasionally.

4. As the mixture begins to set, take the pan off the heat and quickly scatter the mushroom and tomato over the top. Add the strips of red pepper and cover with grated cheese.

5. Put the pan under a hot grill. The mixture will rise and become a golden brown. (Be careful not to burn the handle of the pan.)

6. Do not fold the omelette; slide it from the pan onto a hot dish and serve quickly.

Smoked Haddock and Mushroom Omelette

For 4

½ lb smoked haddock	*2 oz butter*
¼ pint white sauce	*6 eggs*
1 tablespoon lemon juice	*1 hard-boiled egg*
6 oz mushrooms	

1. Poach the fish in salted water until tender.
2. Remove skin and bones and flake the fish with a fork.
3. Mix the fish with the white sauce and season with salt, pepper and lemon juice.
4. Slice the mushrooms and cook in 1½ oz butter for 3 minutes. Mix with the fish mixture.
5. Make 1 large or 4 small omelettes and slide onto a hot serving dish.
6. Put the fish mixture on top of the omelette and fold in half.
7. Serve immediately garnished with sliced hard-boiled egg.

Welsh Rarebit with Mushrooms

For 2

2 oz butter	*4 oz cheese (grated)*
½ teaspoon mustard	*2 slices toast*
pinch Cayenne pepper	*4 oz open mushrooms*

1. Melt 1 oz butter in a pan then remove from the heat.
2. Stir in mustard, cayenne and a pinch of salt.
3. Add the cheese and stir thoroughly to make a spreading consistency.
4. Spread one side of each slice of toast with the mixture.
5. Heat the remaining butter in the grill pan and grill the mushrooms.
6. Put the Welsh Rarebit under the hot grill until golden. Top with the mushrooms and serve at once.

Cheese and Crabmeat Rolls

For 4

8 small bread rolls	*½ pint cheese sauce*
1 oz butter	*6 oz crabmeat*
½ lb mushrooms (sliced)	*salad vegetables*

1. Put the rolls in a cool oven to warm through.

2. Heat the butter in a pan and fry the mushrooms for 4 minutes. Season with salt and pepper during cooking.

3. Stir the mushrooms into the hot cheese sauce. Check seasoning.

4. Cut the tops off the rolls and scoop out the centres. Spread the inside of each with crabmeat and return the rolls to the oven for a few moments.

5. When ready to serve; fill each roll with hot mushroom cheese sauce and serve with a fresh salad.

1746755

Cod Roe Castles

For 4

1 7 oz tin cod roes
1 egg
breadcrumbs
shallow fat for frying

4 large open mushrooms (or more smaller ones)
4 rounds buttered toast
1 tin tomato sauce

1. Cut the roes into four slices. Coat with egg and breadcrumbs and fry in hot shallow fat until golden. Drain on kitchen paper and keep warm.

2. Fry the mushrooms, season with salt and pepper and cook for about 4 minutes.

3. Place each mushroom on a round of buttered toast. Put the cod roe on top and pour over the hot tomato sauce.

Sardine Savouries

For 4

3 oz butter
12 large cups mushrooms
2 tins sardines in oil

3 tablespoons tomato ketchup
paprika
hot buttered toast

1. Heat 2 oz butter in the grill pan and grill the mushrooms for about 4 minutes.

2. Mash the sardines. Heat the rest of the butter and the tomato ketchup in a pan. Add the sardines and season with salt and paprika.
3. Spoon the sardine mixture on top of the mushrooms.
4. Place under a moderate grill for 2–3 minutes.
5. Serve with fingers of hot buttered toast.

Herring Roes on Toast

For 4

¾ lb mushrooms (sliced)	3–4 oz butter
juice of ½ lemon	4 large squares hot buttered
1½ lb soft herring roes	toast
seasoned flour	wedges of lemon

1. Slice the mushrooms and sprinkle with lemon juice, salt and pepper.
2. Turn the roes in seasoned flour.
3. Heat some of the butter in a frying pan and fry the mushrooms for about 4 minutes. Remove from the pan and keep hot.
4. Fry the roes in hot butter until golden brown.
5. Cover the squares of hot buttered toast with mushrooms and arrange the roes on top. Garnish with wedges of lemon.

Mushroom Muffins

For 4

4 muffins	butter
4 portions Boursin herb	8 open mushrooms
cheese	4 tomatoes (halved)

1. Split the muffins in half and grill until golden brown.
2. Spread the muffins with the herb cheese.
3. Grill the mushrooms, dipping in hot butter.

4. Grill the tomatoes, brushed with butter and seasoned with salt and pepper.

5. When ready to serve, put the muffins under the grill, as the cheese melts place a mushroom on top and cap with the grilled tomatoes.

Many different toppings can be used for this dish which is ideal for a teenage party.

Gouda Castles

For 2-3

1 oz butter
1 small onion (chopped)
4 oz button mushrooms (sliced)
1 dessertspoon tomato paste

4 tablespoons double cream
4 oz Gouda cheese (grated)
6 rounds bread (fried or toasted)
parsley (chopped)

1. Heat the butter in a pan and lightly fry the onion until golden.
2. Add the mushrooms, cook for a minute then stir in the tomato paste and cream. Season well and allow to simmer for 5 minutes.
3. Remove from the heat and stir in the cheese. Check seasoning.
4. Pile the mixture on the rounds of bread and put under a hot grill until golden.
5. Garnish with parsley and serve immediately.

Starters

HORS D'OEUVRES, cocktails, soups, pâtés etc.: serve small portions as an appetiser to a meal. Many of these dishes will be found suitable for light meals when the number of portions shown on the recipe should be halved.

Pink Clouds

For 4–6

1 lb small button mushrooms
½ clove garlic
¼ pint cream
2 tablespoons mayonnaise

4 tablespoons tomato ketchup
½ teaspoon Worcestershire sauce
1 lettuce

1. Wash and dry the mushrooms; cut any larger ones in half.
2. Crush the garlic finely. Whip the cream lightly.
3. Mix mayonnaise, ketchup, Worcestershire sauce and cream. Add garlic, salt and pepper and stir well.
4. Turn the mushrooms in the dressing* and serve on a bed of shredded lettuce in hors d'oeuvre glasses.

*Do not mix the mushrooms with the dressing more than 30 minutes before serving or the texture of the sauce will be spoilt.

Pink Clouds Avocado

For 6

Follow the recipe for Pink Clouds and spoon the mixture on halves of Avocado pear. For six people allow 3 pears; halve and remove the stones before filling. Chill well before serving.

White Grape Cocktail

For 4

½ lb white grapes   *1 carton natural yogurt*
3 oz button mushrooms   *1 teaspoon mint (chopped)*

1. Remove the skin and pips from the grapes. Cut grapes in half.
2. Finely slice the mushrooms.
3. When ready to serve, stir the grapes and mushrooms into the chilled yogurt and serve in glasses. Sprinkle each portion with a little chopped mint.

Marinaded Mushrooms

For 4–6

1 tablespoon vinegar   *4 tablespoons tomato juice*
1 tablespoon lemon juice   *1 tablespoon parsley*
1 tablespoon oil   *(chopped)*
1 teaspoon onion (grated)   *salt and ground black pepper*
½ *teaspoon Worcestershire*   *1 lb button mushrooms*
  sauce

1. Put all the ingredients except the mushrooms into a sealed container or screw-top jar. Shake well. Taste for seasoning.
2. Turn the mushrooms in the dressing. Seal and leave to stand in a cool place for 24 hours if possible. Gently turn the mushrooms from time to time.
3. Serve with slices of brown bread and butter.

Mushrooms à la Grecque

For 6

3 tablespoons olive oil
4 oz onion (*chopped*)
¼ pint dry white wine
1¼ lb small button mush-
  rooms
½ lb tomatoes (*skinned,
  seeded and chopped*)

black pepper
*2 bay leaves
*2 cloves garlic (*chopped*)
*2 sprigs parsley
*½ teaspoon thyme
parsley (*chopped*)

1. Heat the oil in a pan, add the onion and cook until tender and just turning brown.
2. Pour in the wine. Add mushrooms and tomato; sprinkle with plenty of salt and freshly ground black pepper.
3. Put all the starred herbs into a muslin, tie and put into the pan.
4. Cook uncovered for about 20 minutes. The liquid will reduce and thicken during cooking.
5. Remove the herb muslin.
6. Serve chilled, sprinkled with a little chopped parsley.

Thousand Island Dreams

For 6–8

¾ lb button mushrooms
½ cucumber
1 bottle Thousand Island
  dressing

4 oz prawns (*peeled*)
1 cos lettuce
mint

1. Dice mushrooms and cucumber; coat with dressing.
2. Add most of the prawns and check seasoning.
3. Arrange the mixture on 8 lettuce leaves and set on a dish.
4. Garnish each portion with remaining prawns and a sprig of fresh mint.

Jellied Mushrooms

For 6

6 oz button mushrooms	*few drops Angostura Bitters*
1 large tin Consommé	*1 teaspoon gelatin*
1 teaspoon Soy sauce	*1–2 lemons*
½ teaspoon Worcestershire	*1 tablespoon brandy*
sauce	*squares of toasted bread*

1. Put the mushrooms, soup, sauces and bitters into a pan.
2. Simmer gently for about 6 minutes when the mushrooms should be tender but not soft.
3. Dissolve the gelatin in 2 tablespoons of hot water. Pour into the mushroom pan.
4. Season with salt, pepper, lemon juice and brandy.
5. Turn into a shallow dish. Arrange the mushrooms with the stalks upwards; the jelly will not necessarily completely cover the mushrooms.
6. Put into the refrigerator until set.
7. Cut into sections with a knife. Just before serving, set on squares of crisp toast. Serve with lemon wedges.

Liver Suzanne

For 4

Dressing:

1 tablespoon Mango chutney	*3 oz button mushrooms*
2 tablespoons olive oil	*2 oz gherkins*
1 tablespoon wine vinegar	*4 spring onions*
½ teaspoon French mustard	*2 inches cucumber*
¾ lb mixed Continental	*1 red pimento (tinned)*
sausages (sliced)	

1. Dressing: Sieve the chutney, put into a screw-top jar with the oil, vinegar and mustard. Season with salt and pepper. Seal and shake vigorously. Chill until ready for use.

2. Chop the remaining ingredients and mix together.
3. Put the sliced meats onto a dish and top with a little of the vegetable mixture.
4. Pour over the dressing when ready to serve.

Mortadella Rolls

For 4

3 inches cucumber	4 thin slices large Mortadella
3 oz button mushrooms	sausage
4 oz cream cheese	lettuce
paprika	gherkins

1. Finely dice the cucumber and mushrooms. Sprinkle with plenty of salt and leave to stand for 1 hour.
2. Drain the water from the cucumber and mushrooms. Mix these with the cream cheese. Season with paprika.
3. Spread the mixture on the slices of Mortadella sausage. Roll-up the sausages and wrap in foil.
4. Chill in the freezer part of the refrigerator for about 45 minutes.
5. Serve on a lettuce leaf and garnish with gherkins.

Anchovy Cream Mushrooms

For 6–8

$\frac{1}{2}$ lb small button mush-rooms	squares of fresh brown bread and butter
1 oz anchovy fillets	anchovy fillets (garnish)
4 oz cream cheese	parsley (chopped)
paprika	

1. Pull out the stalks of the mushrooms and put these aside for use in another dish.
2. Pound the anchovy fillets and mix with the cream cheese.

3. Season with paprika and mix well.
4. Spread the inside of each mushroom with the mixture.
5. Garnish with a small piece of anchovy fillet and sprinkle with chopped parsley.
6. Chill the mushrooms until ready to serve.
7. Serve each mushroom on a square of brown bread and butter.

Smoked Salmon Savouries

For 6

18 button mushrooms	*1 teaspoon horseradish*
1 lemon	*cream*
3 oz smoked salmon (odd pieces if available)	*2 tablespoons cream (whipped)*
2 hard-boiled eggs	*black pepper*
	parsley (chopped)

1. Pull out the stalks of the mushrooms and put these aside for use in another dish.
2. Put the mushrooms into boiling salted water, seasoned with lemon juice and cook for 1 minute. Drain and dry on kitchen paper.
3. Put the salmon, egg yolks, horseradish and cream into a blender and mix until creamy. Season with salt and freshly ground black pepper to taste.
4. Fill the mushrooms with the mixture and serve on a bed of chopped hard-boiled egg whites sprinkled with grated lemon rind and chopped parsley.

Porchester Prawns

For 8

2 oz butter	*6 oz prawns (peeled)*
8 large cup mushrooms	*¼ pint double cream*
black pepper	*Parmesan cheese*

1. Heat the butter in the grill pan; turn the mushroom caps in the butter and grill for 3 minutes each side. Season well with salt and freshly ground black pepper during cooking.
2. Fill the mushrooms with the prawns. Pour over a little cream and sprinkle with Parmesan cheese.
3. Grill under a moderate grill until a light golden colour then serve at once with slices of fresh brown bread and butter.

Mussels Continental Style

For 6

2 quarts mussels
½ pint fish stock
1 teaspoon wine vinegar
2 bay leaves
2 slices onion
10 oz mushrooms (sliced)
4 oz butter

black pepper
1 clove garlic (crushed)
2 tablespoons parsley
    (chopped)
4 tablespoons dried bread-
    crumbs

1. Clean the mussels thoroughly and put into a large pan. Add stock, vinegar, bay leaves and sliced onion. Cover tightly and cook until mussels have opened: 3–4 minutes.
2. Remove the mussels from their shells.
3. Turn the mushrooms in 1 oz hot butter. Season well with salt and freshly ground black pepper. Cook for 2 minutes over a fierce heat.
4. Mix the mushrooms and mussels and put into individual ovenproof dishes.
5. Melt the rest of the butter in a pan; add the crushed garlic and chopped parsley. Simmer for a minute.
6. Pour the garlic butter into the dishes and top the ingredients with breadcrumbs.
7. Bake in oven 400 degrees F, mark 6 for 15 minutes.

Mussels Portugaises

For 6–8

2 quarts mussels
½ pint white wine or dry
 cider
2 bay leaves
1 small onion
1 oz butter
2 tablespoons oil
4 oz button mushrooms
 (quartered)

2 oz shallot (chopped)
1 clove garlic (crushed)
1 tablespoon parsley
 (chopped)
1 lb tomatoes (skinned,
 quartered and seeded)
black pepper
1 lemon

1. Clean the mussels thoroughly and put into a large pan. Add wine, bay leaves and sliced onion. Cover tightly and cook until mussels have opened: 3–4 minutes.
2. Keep the stock and remove the mussels from their shells.
3. Heat the butter and oil in a shallow pan, add the mushrooms and cook over a fierce heat for 3 minutes. Remove the mushrooms from the pan.
4. Put the shallots, garlic and parsley into the pan, cook for a minute, then add the tomatoes. Season with salt and freshly ground black pepper, simmer for 15 minutes.
5. Pour the wine stock into the pan and put in the mussels and mushrooms.
6. Cover the pan and cook gently for 20 minutes.
7. Turn into a hot serving dish; garnish with wedges of lemon. Serve with brown bread and butter.

Crêpes à la Champignon

For 6

½ pint pancake batter
6 oz mushrooms
2 oz butter
1 oz flour
¼ pint meat stock

1 teaspoon lemon juice
2 tablespoons double cream
6 oz lean cooked meat or
 poultry (diced)

1. Make 6 small pancakes, keep warm.
2. Cook 4 oz sliced mushrooms in hot butter for 1 minute.
3. Stir in the flour, add stock and lemon juice; bring to the boil and thin with cream.
4. Add the meat, check seasoning and simmer for 3 minutes.
5. Spoon the mixture onto the pancakes, fold each in four making a triangular shape.
6. Garnish with whole fried mushrooms.

Veal Vitesse

For 6

4 oz pie veal	*1 oz Gouda cheese (grated)*
4 oz mushrooms	*1 tablespoon parsley*
bay leaf	*(chopped)*
4 oz chopped ham	*1–2 eggs (beaten)*
2 level teaspoons gelatin	*breadcrumbs*
1 oz butter	*deep fat for frying*
1 oz flour	*1 lemon*
3 tablespoons milk	

1. Chop the veal and mushrooms, put into a pan and barely cover with water. Season with salt, pepper and bay leaf. Cook gently until tender.
2. Strain off $\frac{1}{4}$ pint stock. Mince the veal and mushrooms together with the chopped ham.
3. Melt the gelatin in a little of the veal stock.
4. Make a thick white sauce with the butter, flour, milk and rest of the $\frac{1}{4}$ pint stock. Season, bring to the boil and simmer for 2 minutes.
5. Stir the gelatin, meats and mushrooms, cheese and parsley into the sauce.
6. Spread on a plate, refrigerate until completely cold and firm to touch.
7. Shape into small balls on a floured board. Coat in beaten egg

and breadcrumbs. Fry in hot deep fat until golden. Drain on kitchen paper.

8. Serve piping hot with wedges of lemon.

Liver and Mushroom Pâté

1 onion (chopped)
1 clove garlic (crushed)
3 oz butter
6 oz mushrooms
8 oz liver
4 rashers fatty bacon

1 tablespoon parsley
(chopped)
1 bay leaf
pinch thyme
black pepper

1. Soften the onion and garlic in 1 oz hot butter.
2. Chop the mushrooms and add to the pan. Season with salt, cover and simmer for 2 minutes.
3. Add the liver, thinly sliced, and the bacon and sauté for 3 minutes. Sprinkle with herbs and seasonings; cook for 5 minutes.
4. Cool, then chop and mince until the mixture is fine.
5. Melt remaining butter and stir into the mixture.
6. Turn into a mould and chill until ready to serve.

Pork Pâté with Brandy

4 oz mushrooms
2 lb belly of pork
½ lb pig's liver
1 tablespoon onion (chopped)
1 teaspoon mixed herbs
1 tablespoon parsley
(chopped)

1½ tablespoons flour
½ teaspoon salt
¼ teaspoon ground black
pepper
2 eggs
2 teaspoons Angostura Bitters
2 teaspoons brandy

1. Blanch the mushrooms in salted water for 1 minute. Drain and dry on kitchen paper.
2. Cut the meats finely and put through a mincer twice.
3. Blend the meats, onion and herbs together in an electric blender or through a strong sieve.
4. Stir in the flour, salt and pepper. Add the beaten eggs, Angostura Bitters and brandy; mix thoroughly.
5. Turn half the mixture into a greased pâté dish or loaf tin. Put the mushrooms into the tin, cover with the remaining meat mixture and press down with a wooden spatula.
7. Bake in oven 350 degrees F, mark 4 for 1½–2 hours. The fat should be clear of meat juices when the pâté is cooked.
8. Cool under an even weight. Serve chilled.

Cold Prawn and Mushroom Bisque

For 6

½ lb prawns (peeled)   1 tablespoon tomato paste
4 oz button mushrooms   1 heaped teaspoon curry
1 pint good fish stock   powder
1½ oz butter   ½ pint cream
1½ oz flour

1. Put aside a few prawns and slices of mushroom for garnish.
2. Put prawns and sliced mushrooms into a pan with the stock. Simmer for 3 minutes.
3. Put into a blender or through a sieve until the mixture is a fine purée.
4. Make a roux with the butter and flour, add the stock and prawn mixture. Stir in tomato paste and bring to the boil. Then put aside to cool.
5. Stir in the curry powder and cream. Check seasoning. Chill until ready to serve.
6. Serve in individual dishes garnished with mushroom slices and prawns.

Iced Paprika Cream

For 4–6

6 oz button mushrooms	5 oz carton soured cream
½ clove garlic	lemon juice
1 dessertspoon vegetable oil	paprika
5 oz carton plain yogurt	parsley (chopped)

1. Slice the mushrooms, put a few slices aside for garnish. Crush the garlic finely.
2. Put the mushrooms and garlic with the oil into a blender or through a grinder. The mixture should become a purée.
3. Blend in the yogurt and soured cream.
4. Add salt and plenty of lemon juice and paprika to taste.
5. Serve well chilled, garnished with mushroom slices and a little chopped parsley.

Consommé with Mushrooms

For 4

½ lb button mushrooms	1 lemon
1 large can good Consommé soup	

1. Slice the smallest mushroom, sprinkle it with salt and put aside for garnish.
2. Slice all the remaining mushrooms, put into a pan, sprinkle liberally with salt, cover with a lid and heat very gently until all the juice has been extracted; this will take 7–10 minutes and the heat must be kept low all the time.
3. Heat the soup in another pan, add mushroom juice and lemon juice, salt and pepper to taste.
4. Serve piping hot, garnished with the sliced mushroom and lemon wedges.

5. For a special occasion, add a tablespoon of Sherry.

Alternatively, serve the Consommé iced; make as above but put more slices of mushroom aside at the beginning and put these into the soup at the end of preparation. Then chill until the soup sets and serve with lemon wedges.

Cream of Mushroom Soup

For 6

1½ *pints milk*	*2 shallots*
1 bay leaf	*1½ oz butter*
1 blade mace	*1¼ oz flour*
2 sprigs parsley	*3 tablespoon double cream*
1 small carrot	*1 egg yolk*
¾ *lb mushrooms*	*Fried croûtons*

1. Scald the milk with the bay leaf, mace, parsley and carrot. Leave to stand.
2. Put the mushrooms and shallot through the mincer using a fine blade.
3. Heat the butter in a large pan, add the vegetables, sprinkle with plenty of salt and pepper and cook for 5 minutes, stirring frequently.
4. Stir in the flour and blend well.
5. Add the milk, strained, and cook, stirring all the time until the mixture thickens.
6. Pass the mixture through a sieve into a clean saucepan. Heat gently, check seasoning and stir in the cream and beaten egg yolk.
7. Serve really hot (but not boiling), garnishing with fried croûtons.

Fish Soup with Mushrooms

For 6–8

2 lb fish (mixed varieties)	*thyme*
4 tablespoons oil	*bay leaf*
2 tomatoes	*pinch saffron*
2 onions	*3 pints water*
2 cloves garlic	*3 oz Gruyère cheese (grated)*
6 oz mushrooms	

1. Clean the fish and cut into pieces.
2. Heat the oil in a large pan; add fish, tomatoes, sliced onion, crushed garlic, 4 oz sliced mushrooms, thyme, bay leaf, saffron, salt and pepper.
3. Cook for 3 minutes over a moderate heat, stirring all the time.
4. Pour in water, cook for 30 minutes; skim the surface occasionally.
5. Strain the soup through a fine sieve into a clean pan.
6. Finely slice the remaining mushrooms and add to the pan. Simmer for 5 minutes; check seasoning.
7. Pour into a hot serving dish. Serve with Gruyère cheese in a separate bowl.

Potage au Pierre

For 4–6

1 oz butter	*½ lb mushrooms (minced)*
2 tablespoons onion (minced)	*½ pint light stock*
1 tablespoon chives (minced)	*¼ pint cream*
4 tablespoons mashed potato	*1 tablespoon chives (finely*
½ pint scalded milk	*chopped)*

Jellied Meat Ring (page 121) and, in the smaller dishes from the top, Pink Pearls (page 93), Mushroom and Cottage Cheese Salad (page 92), Pink Clouds (page 41) and Curried Cream Salad (page 87).

1. Stir the butter, onion and chives into the potato. Add the milk and cook over a low heat.
2. Cook the minced mushrooms in the stock for 3 minutes. Season with salt and pepper.
3. Combine the contents of the two pans.
4. Add the cream, check seasoning. Serve hot sprinkled with chives.

Casseroled Steak (page 141) and Lemon and Mushroom Soup (page 134).

Family Fillers

MAIN DISHES suitable for all ages. All the recipes are designed to give a nutritionally balanced menu served with fresh vegetables.

Coley Casserole

For 4

1 lb potatoes (peeled)	*½ lb carrots (sliced)*
1½ lb coley (or other white fish)	*½ lb mushrooms (sliced)*
	2 tablespoons parsley (chopped)
4 oz butter	
½ lb onion (sliced)	*¾ pint fish stock*

1. Cut the potatoes to about the size of an egg. Drop into boiling salted water for 3 minutes, then drain.
2. Cut the fish into four portions; season with salt and pepper. Cook in hot butter for about 30 seconds each side. Put fish aside.
3. Put onions and carrots into the pan and cook for 3 minutes over a moderate heat. Remove from the pan.
4. Toss sliced mushrooms and parsley in the remaining butter for 1 minute.
5. Put potatoes into the bottom of an ovenproof dish, cover with onion and carrot, then place the fish on top and scatter the mushrooms and parsley over the whole dish.
6. Pour in well-seasoned fish stock and cover the dish with a lid or cooking foil.
7. Cook in oven 375 degrees F, mark 5 for about 45 minutes.

Cod Bombay

For 4

> 1½ lb cod fillet
> 1 level tablespoon curry
>   powder
> 1 tablespoon flour
> 1 lb mushrooms
> 1 small onion

> 1 egg
> 4 oz butter
> 1 level tablespoon cornflour
> ½ pint fish stock
> parsley

1. Cut the fish into 2-inch squares. Mix 1 teaspoon curry powder with 1 tablespoon flour. Turn the fish in the seasoned flour.
2. Mince or finely chop the mushrooms and onion. Put into a pan without fat, season well and simmer gently until all the moisture has evaporated.
3. Beat the egg, stir into the mushroom mixture and return to the heat for a few moments. Turn into a hot serving dish.
4. Melt 2 oz butter in a pan and blend in the curry powder and cornflour, then add the fish stock. Bring to the boil and simmer for about 3 minutes.
5. Cook the coated fish squares in hot butter.
6. Arrange the fish on the mushroom mixture. Coat with curry sauce and garnish with parsley.

Cod Capers

For 4

> 1½ lb cod fillet
> 4 oz butter
> ¼ pint milk
> 1 lemon

> 1 heaped tablespoon capers
> 12 oz mushrooms
> 2 slices toasted white bread
> 1–2 hard-boiled eggs

1. Poach the fish in water, season with salt and pepper. When cooked, drain and remove skin and bones.
2. Flake the fish and stir in 2 oz butter. Heat milk and gradually add to the fish. A tablespoon of double cream may also be added if liked. Season with lemon juice and stir in the capers.

3. Heat the remaining butter in a pan and fry the mushrooms; season with salt and pepper.
4. Select a few mushrooms for garnish, then line a hot entrée dish with the rest. Turn the fish mixture into the dish.
5. Edge the dish with triangles of toast and slices of hard-boiled egg. Finish with the selected mushrooms.

Cod Crumble

For 4

1½ lb cod fillet
1 bay leaf
3 oz butter
4 oz fresh white bread-
   crumbs

1 onion (chopped)
1 tablespoon parsley
   (chopped)
½ lb open mushrooms
1½ oz butter (melted)

1. Put the fish into a pan of water; add bay leaf, salt and pepper. When fish is cooked, drain, remove skin and bones, then flake the fish.
2. Heat 2 oz butter in a pan, add the breadcrumbs and fry until golden. Remove from pan.
3. Heat 1 oz of butter in the pan, add onion and cook until tender. Mix with the breadcrumbs and chopped parsley.
4. Put half the mixture into an ovenproof dish, add flaked fish and cover with the rest of the breadcrumbs mixture.
5. Arrange the mushrooms stalk downwards over the top of the dish. Brush with melted butter and sprinkle with salt.
6. Bake in oven 375 degrees F, mark 5 for about 20 minutes.

Tomato Fish Tumble

For 4

1 lb mushrooms
1 teaspoon lemon juice
1 tablespoon onion (finely
   chopped)
1½ lb white fish

1 pint tomato pulp
2 oz celery (sliced)
2 oz cucumber (finely diced)
1 tablespoon parsley
   (chopped)

1. Slice mushrooms, mix with lemon juice and onion, season with salt and pepper. Turn into an ovenproof dish.
2. Divide fish into portions and put on top of the mushrooms. Sprinkle with salt and pepper.
3. Put tomato pulp, celery and cucumber into a pan. Cook until vegetables have softened and tomato reduced by one third.
4. Pour over the fish and bake in oven 400 degrees F, mark 6 for about 25 minutes. Garnish with chopped parsley.

Fillets of Plaice with Mushroom Butter Sauce

For 4

4 fillets of plaice	1 lemon
4 oz butter	salt and freshly ground
3 shallots (finely sliced)	black pepper
6 oz button mushrooms	parsley (chopped)
(finely sliced)	

1. Season the fish, dot with a little butter and wrap in a foil packet. Cook in a steamer for about 25 minutes.
2. Melt the rest of the butter in a pan, add the shallots and simmer gently.
3. After a minute add the mushrooms, juice of $\frac{1}{2}$ lemon and plenty of seasoning.
4. Cook gently until all the ingredients are tender.
5. Arrange the fish on a hot serving dish and pour over the sauce. Sprinkle with chopped parsley and garnish with wedges of lemon.

Creamed Tuna Bake

For 4

1 lb dried haricot beans	1 oz Parmesan cheese
1 7 oz tin Tuna steak	(grated)
3 tablespoons double cream	2 oz Gruyère cheese (grated)
(or white sauce)	1 tablespoon dried bread-
$\frac{1}{2}$ lb open mushrooms	crumbs

1. Soak the beans in water over night, then cook in boiling salted water until tender.
2. Drain beans and force through a coarse sieve.
3. Mash the Tuna fish and mix with the sieved beans. Stir in the cream and season well with salt and pepper. Turn into a buttered ovenproof dish.
4. Place the mushrooms, stalks downwards, all over the dish and sprinkle with the cheeses and breadcrumbs.
5. Bake in oven 350 degrees F, mark 4 for about 25 minutes.

Buckingham Beef

For 4

2 oz dripping	$\frac{1}{2}$ lb mushrooms (sliced)
4 oz onion (chopped)	2 standard eggs
$1\frac{1}{2}$ lb minced beef	1 5 oz carton soured cream
1 tablespoon tomato paste	$\frac{1}{2}$ teaspoon paprika
$\frac{1}{2}$ pint brown stock	

1. Heat some dripping in a shallow pan and fry the onion until tender.
2. Add the minced beef and stir well over a moderate heat for about 2 minutes.
3. Add tomato paste, salt and pepper and enough stock to moisten the meat.
4. Turn into an ovenproof dish.
5. Turn the sliced mushrooms in hot dripping, season well with salt and pepper.
6. Arrange the mushrooms on top of the meat.
7. Beat the eggs, soured cream, paprika and a little salt together. Pour over the dish.
8. Bake in oven 350 degrees F, mark 4 for about 30 minutes or until the custard is set.

Roast Beef with Horseradish Cups

For 6

> *joint of roast beef*   *3 oz cream cheese*
> *1 teaspoon horseradish*   *paprika*
>   *(grated)*   *12 cup mushrooms*

1. Roast the beef in a roasting tin in a moderate oven. Time according to weight.
2. Cream together the horseradish and cream cheese. Season with salt and paprika.
3. Spread a little of the horseradish cream in each of the mushrooms and place them in the roasting tin round the joint for the last 15 minutes of roasting time.

Beef Stew with Mushroom Dumplings

For 4

> *1¼ lb stewing steak*   *gravy powder*
> *seasoned flour*   *½ teaspoon mixed herbs*
> *2 oz dripping*   *1 bay leaf*
> *2 onions (sliced)*
> *2 oz chopped bacon pieces*   Dumplings:
> *½ lb mushrooms*   *8 oz flour*
> *1 pint stock*   *4 oz suet*
> *1 teaspoon tomato paste*

1. Cut the meat into 1-inch cubes, toss in seasoned flour and seal in hot dripping.
2. Put the meat into a casserole and add the onion and bacon.
3. Put four mushrooms aside and quarter the rest, then add these to the casserole.
4. Season the stock with tomato paste, gravy powder, mixed herbs, bay leaf, salt and pepper and pour into the dish.
5. Cover the casserole and cook in oven 350 degrees F, mark 4 for about 2½ hours.

6. Prepare the dumplings; mix together the flour, ½ teaspoon salt and suet. Bind with cold water to form a soft dough.
7. Halve the mushrooms, cover each with dough to form 8 small dumplings. Put into the stew and cook for a further 25 minutes.

Steak, Kidney and Mushroom Pie

For 4

1 lb stewing steak	*¾ pint brown stock*
4 oz kidney	*bouquet garni*
seasoned flour	*½ lb mushrooms*
3 tablespoons oil	*½ lb rough puff pastry*
2 medium onions (sliced)	*beaten egg (or milk)*

1. Cut the steak and kidney into cubes. Turn in seasoned flour.
2. Heat the oil in a pan and turn the meats in the oil until well sealed.
3. Add the onion to the pan. Season with salt and pepper, pour in the stock and add the bouquet garni.
4. Cover with a well-fitting lid and allow to simmer gently for 1½ hours.
5. Quarter the mushrooms, mix with the meat and turn all into a pie dish.
6. Cover with the pastry, brush with egg or milk.
7. Bake in oven 400 degrees F, mark 6 for about 40 minutes.

Mushroom and Oxtail Supreme

For 4

1 oxtail cut into 2-inch pieces	*½ pint good stock*
2 oz dripping	*¼ pint light ale*
½ lb onions (finely chopped)	*bouquet garni*
1 tablespoon tomato paste	*½ lb open mushrooms*

1. Cook the oxtail in hot dripping until browned on all sides. Put into a casserole. Turn the onions in the fat for a few moments, then put these into the casserole.
2. Mix the tomato paste with stock and beer and pour into the dish.
3. Season and add the bouquet garni.
4. Cover with a well-fitting lid, cook in oven 325 degrees F, mark 3 for $2\frac{1}{2}$ hours.
5. Put mushrooms into the casserole and baste with stock; replace lid and continue cooking for another hour.
6. Remove the bay leaf and serve with hot fresh vegetables.

For special occasions use $\frac{1}{2}$ bottle red wine instead of beer.

Meat Cakes in Sweet Pepper Sauce

For 4

12 oz roast meat (minced)	*1 oz green pepper (finely*
1 teaspoon onion (grated)	*sliced)*
½ teaspoon mixed herbs	*½ lb mushrooms (finely*
½ lb mashed potato	*sliced)*
seasoned flour	*2 oz butter*
fat for shallow frying	*¼ pint tomato pulp*
Sauce:	*¼ pint dry cider*
1 small onion	*parsley (chopped)*

1. Mix the meat, grated onion and herbs with enough potato to bind the mixture together. Add salt and pepper during the mixing
2. Shape mixture into round cakes, turn in seasoned flour and fry in hot shallow fat on both sides.
3. To prepare the sauce: slice the onion finely and cook with the green pepper and mushrooms in hot butter until all the ingredients are tender.
4. Stir in the tomato pulp and the cider, season with salt and pepper and cook over a fierce heat so that the liquid reduces by one third.
5. Put the meat cakes onto a hot dish and pour over the sauce. Sprinkle with parsley.

Carlton Cutlets

For 4

4 lamb cutlets	*1 large apple*
4 large open mushrooms	*2 oz cheese (grated)*
2 oz butter	*2 tomatoes*

1. Turn cutlets and mushrooms in melted butter in grill pan.
2. Place cutlets on grid above mushrooms and grill until tender.
3. Grate apple and mix with cheese, fill mushrooms with the mixture.
4. Return to the grill for a minute or two.
5. Serve mushrooms on top of cutlets. Garnish with tomatoes.

Barbecued Leg of Lamb

For 6

1 leg of lamb	$\frac{1}{2}$ *pint tomato pulp*
1 clove of garlic	*1 tablespoon vinegar*
1 teaspoon lemon juice	*1 tablespoon Worcestershire*
grated nutmeg	*sauce*
	4 oz mushrooms (minced)
Sauce:	*bouquet garni*
1 oz butter	$\frac{1}{4}$ *pint apple purée*
1 small onion (chopped)	*1 tablespoon lemon juice*

1. Rub the leg of lamb with a cut clove of garlic. Sprinkle with lemon juice and grated nutmeg.
2. Spit roast or oven roast the joint until tender. Time according to weight.
3. To make the sauce: heat the butter in a pan and add the onion and remaining garlic, finely crushed. Simmer until tender.
4. Stir in the tomato pulp, vinegar, Worcestershire sauce and minced mushrooms. Season with salt, pepper and bouquet garni. Simmer for 3 minutes.

5. Pour the apple purée and lemon juice into the pan and simmer gently for 20 minutes.

6. Put the sauce into a sauce boat and serve with the roast lamb.

Pork and Mushroom Loaf

For 6

1¼ lb lean pork	*black pepper*
1 small onion	*2 eggs*
6 black olives	*2 oz Edam cheese (diced)*
4 oz mushrooms (chopped)	*2 hard-boiled eggs (halved)*
1 clove garlic (crushed)	

1. Mince together the pork, onion and stoned olives. Mix with the chopped mushrooms.

2. Stir in the crushed garlic; season well with salt and freshly ground black pepper. Stir in the beaten eggs.

3. Turn half the mixture into a greased loaf tin. Arrange the cheese and halved hard-boiled eggs on top and cover with the remaining meat.

4. Cover the tin with foil and bake in oven 350 degrees F, mark 4 for 1½ hours.

5. Allow to cool in the tin. When cold, turn onto a meat dish and cut into slices.

Stuffed Loin of Pork

For 4–6

1 large cooking apple	*1 oz butter (melted)*
6 oz fresh breadcrumbs	*½ lemon*
4 oz mushrooms (chopped)	*1 egg*
1½ oz almonds	*1½–2 lb boned loin of pork*

1. Peel, core and chop the apple. Mix the breadcrumbs, apple, mushrooms and almonds together.
2. Season with salt and pepper.
3. Add the melted butter, juice and rind of ½ lemon and bind with beaten egg. Mix well.
4. Cover the boned area of the meat with the stuffing. Roll up the meat and secure with skewers or string.
5. Roast in oven 400 degrees F, mark 6. Check for tenderness at the end of 1 hour.
6. Serve on a hot meat dish.

New York Chicken

For 4

6–8 oz long grain rice	*½ teaspoon mustard*
1 large onion (chopped)	*¼ pint cream*
¾ pint dry white wine	*1 tablespoon capers*
6 oz mushrooms	*1 lb chicken (cooked)*
2 oz butter	*paprika*
1 oz flour	*parsley (chopped)*

1. Cook the rice in boiling salted water. When tender, drain well.
2. Put the onion and wine into a pan and simmer for 10 minutes.
4. Slice the mushrooms and cook in hot butter for 3 minutes. Stir in the flour and cook for 1 minute.
4. Blend in the wine and onion and bring to the boil. Season.
5. Reduce the heat and stir in the mustard, cream and capers. Simmer very gently for 5 minutes.
6. Cut the chicken into 1-inch cubes and add to the sauce. Cook for a further 5 minutes.
7. Put the rice onto a hot meat dish and turn the chicken into the centre. Sprinkle with paprika and parsley.

Mushroom and Bacon Stuffing for Turkey

For 10–12 lb bird

1 teaspoon mixed herbs
1 tablespoon parsley
  (chopped)
1 dessertspoon onion
  (chopped)
6 oz fresh white bread-
  crumbs

½ teaspoon garlic salt
6 oz streaky bacon (chopped)
8 oz mushrooms (chopped)
2 oz butter (melted)
3 eggs (beaten)

1. Mix the herbs, parsley and onion with the breadcrumbs.
2. Season with garlic salt and pepper.
3. Stir in the bacon and mushrooms.
4. Bind with melted butter and beaten eggs.
5. Fill the body of the turkey with the mixture.
6. Roast the turkey in the usual way.

Mushroom Pudding

For 4

½–¾ lb mushrooms
2 teaspoons lemon juice
½ lb self-raising flour
¼ lb suet

1 tablespoon onion (finely
  chopped)
½ teaspoon sage

1. Quarter the mushrooms. Sprinkle with salt and lemon juice and leave to stand in a cool place.
2. Put the flour and ½ teaspoon salt into a bowl. Stir in the chopped suet and bind to a soft dough with cold water.
3. Line a 2-pint pudding basin with three-quarters of the dough.
4. Mix the mushrooms, onion and sage and fill the basin with this mixture. Pack the ingredients tightly, as they will shrink during cooking.

5. Damp the edges of the pastry and cover with a lid of the remaining dough.
6. Cover with foil and steam for 2½ hours.

Mushrooms in the Hole

For 4

4 oz flour   ½ oz lard
1 egg   ½ lb cup mushrooms
½ pint milk

1. Make a pouring batter with the flour, egg and milk. Season with salt and beat well. Leave to stand for at least 30 minutes.
2. Heat the lard in an ovenproof dish in oven 450 degrees F, mark 8.
3. Put the mushrooms into the hot fat and pour over the batter.
4. Bake in oven for about 40 minutes, reducing the oven temperature to 400 degrees F, mark 6 after 20 minutes.

Batter Bake

For 4

1½ oz dripping   ½ lb cooked meat (diced)
1 onion (chopped)   ½ lb tomatoes (sliced)
½ lb mushrooms (sliced)   ½ pint pouring batter
½ green pepper (finely
    sliced)

1. Heat some dripping in a frying pan. Add the onion, mushrooms and green pepper. Season and cook over a moderate heat for 4 minutes.
2. Put a knob of dripping into an ovenproof dish and place dish in oven 425 degrees F, mark 7.

3. Mix the vegetables with the cooked meat and sliced tomatoes.
4. Stir in the batter and pour all these ingredients into the hot dish.
5. Bake in oven for 20 minutes, then reduce the temperature to 375 degrees F, mark 5 and cook for a further 20 minutes or until the mixture is evenly set.

Glazed Savoury Roll

For 4

1½ lb potatoes (boiled)
1 oz butter
2 tablespoons milk
2 eggs (beaten)
3 tablespoons oil
½ lb mushrooms (chopped)

4 oz onion (chopped)
1 teaspoon lemon juice
½ teaspoon mixed herbs
10 oz liver
4 tomatoes (skinned and sliced)

1. Cream the potatoes with butter and milk; add nearly all the egg and beat well over a low heat until the mixture is thick and fluffy.
2. Heat the oil in another pan, add onion and mushrooms, season with salt, pepper, lemon juice and mixed herbs and cook for 4 minutes.
3. Add the liver, cut into ¾-inch dice. Turn in the oil until just tender.
4. Spread a good third of the potato on an oblong ovenproof dish.
5. Set the liver and mushroom mixture on top of the potato.
6. Cover with the tomato slices.
7. Use the rest of the potato to cover completely the other ingredients, so making a roll. Make a pattern on the roll with a fork.
8. Bake in oven 400 degrees F, mark 6 for 40 minutes. After 5 minutes take the dish from the oven and brush the top of the potato with the remaining beaten egg.

Chicken Liver Savoury

For 4

8 oz egg noodles
2 oz butter
6 oz chicken livers (chopped)
6 oz mushrooms (sliced)
1 level tablespoon flour

½ pint chicken stock
2 tablespoons white wine
1 tablespoon parsley
   (chopped)
2 tablespoons single cream

1. Cook the noodles according to the instructions on the packet.
2. Melt the butter in a saucepan and gently sauté the livers for 2–3 minutes.
3. Add the mushrooms and sauté for a further 3 minutes.
4. Stir in the flour then gradually add the stock, wine and parsley. Cook for 5 minutes.
5. Just before serving, stir in the cream and heat carefully, making sure that the mixture does not boil.
6. Make a border of the noodles in a hot serving dish and pour the sauce in the centre.

Apple Jacks

For 4

4 large potatoes
2 oz butter
2 tablespoons milk
4 large mushrooms (or 8
   smaller ones)

4 rashers streaky bacon
4 tablespoons apple purée

1. Scrub potatoes, rub skins with fat and bake in oven 400 degrees F, mark 6 for about 1 hour.
2. Cut tops off potatoes and scoop out the centre. Put half the scooped-out potato aside for other use.
3. Mash the rest of the centre potato with a little butter, milk, salt and pepper. Put back into the potato skins and keep warm in a low oven.

4. Fry mushrooms in hot butter; season with salt and pepper.
5. Chop bacon and fry for a minute. Mix bacon with apple purée and heat gently in another pan.
6. Halve the mushrooms and put the cut edges into the potato, then fill the space between the two halves with apple and bacon.
7. Return to the oven for a few minutes to ensure the Apple Jacks are really hot.

Country Style Potatoes

For 4

4 large potatoes　　　　　　*1 tablespoon chives (chopped)*
vegetable oil　　　　　　　*8 oz cream cheese*
6 oz mushrooms　　　　　　*paprika*
1 tablespoon onion (minced)
pinch sage

1. Scrub potatoes and brush with oil.
2. Cook in oven 425 degrees F, mark 7 for about 50 minutes or until soft when pressed.
3. Finely chop mushrooms, mix with the minced onion, season with salt, pepper and sage. Put into a pan (without fat) and cook gently until all the liquid evaporates and the vegetables are tender. Leave aside until cold.
4. Stir mushrooms, onion and chives into the cream cheese. Season well with salt and paprika.
5. Chill cheese mixture until ready to serve.
6. Split hot potatoes and spoon the cheese mixture on the top.

Bacon Custard

For 4

8–10 slices white bread　　　*3 standard eggs*
10 oz bacon rashers (cut in　　*$\frac{3}{4}$ pint milk*
　strips)　　　　　　　　*nutmeg*
$\frac{1}{2}$ lb mushrooms (sliced)　　*3 oz cheese (grated)*

1. Butter an ovenproof dish.
2. Cover the bottom and sides of the dish with slices of bread cut to fit.
3. Put alternate layers of bacon and mushrooms into the dish.
4. Beat the eggs and milk together in a basin. Season well with salt, pepper and nutmeg.
5. Pour into the dish and cover the top with slices of bread.
6. Sprinkle the cheese thickly over the surface.
7. Bake in oven 350 degrees F, mark 4 for about 50 minutes or until the custard is set.

Devilled Kebabs

For 4

12 oz bacon (*not sliced*)
½ lb cup mushrooms
1 green pepper
2 tablespoons lemon juice
2 tablespoons oil
1 teaspoon mustard
1 teaspoon Worcestershire sauce
1 teaspoon brown sugar
4–6 oz Quick macaroni
watercress

1. Cut the bacon into cubes. Blanch the mushrooms in boiling salted water for 30 seconds.
2. Hold the green pepper over the cooker burner until the skin is black. Put into cold water and scrape off the black skin. Cut the pepper into thick slices, removing the core and seeds.
3. Thread the bacon, pepper and mushrooms alternately onto skewers.
4. Mix lemon juice, oil, mustard, Worcestershire sauce and brown sugar together in a pan. Warm gently until all ingredients are well blended.
5. Brush the kebabs with the dressing and cook them under a moderate grill until all the ingredients are tender. Turn the skewers occasionally during cooking and brush with dressing as required.
6. Serve kebabs on a bed of macaroni, cooked according to the instructions on the packet. Garnish with watercress.

Sausage Kebabs with Buttered Noodles

For 4

8 oz curled egg noodles	*4 tomatoes*
8 button onions	*8 button mushrooms*
1 green pepper	*olive oil*
4 chipolata sausages	*1 oz butter*
4 rashers streaky bacon	*1 tin tomato sauce*

1. Cook the egg noodles according to the instructions on the packet.
2. Blanch the onions and green pepper and cut the pepper into 8 pieces, removing the seeds.
3. Divide the chipolatas into 2 by twisting and cutting.
4. Halve the tomatoes and cut the stalks off the mushrooms.
5. Stretch the bacon rashers by spreading with a round-bladed knife; cut into 2 and form into rolls.
6. Place the ingredients alternately onto 4 large skewers, brush with olive oil and season with salt and pepper.
7. Place under a medium grill for about 10 minutes, turning occasionally.
8. Toss the noodles in butter and place on a large hot serving plate. Arrange the skewers on the top and serve hot tomato sauce separately.

Sausage-Meat Horseshoe

For 6

12 oz rough puff pastry	*6 oz mushrooms (finely*
1 lb sausage-meat	*chopped)*
	1 beaten egg

1. Roll the pastry to an oblong shape.
2. Season and mix the mushrooms and sausage-meat together.
3. Make a long sausage with the mixture. Lay it on top of the pastry.
4. Brush the edges of the pastry with beaten egg. Roll up the

pastry round the sausage, making the join in the pastry come underneath.

5. Put the roll onto a baking sheet. Make a number of cuts in the pastry on the side furthest away from you. Bend the roll round to a horseshoe shape.
6. Brush with beaten egg.
7. Bake in oven 400 degrees F, mark 6 for 40 minutes.

Frankfurter Wheel

For 4-5

1 lb cabbage
2 oz onion
2 oz green pepper
¾ lb tomatoes
½ lb mushrooms

2 oz butter
1 tablespoon lemon juice
1 teaspoon paprika
12 oz Frankfurter sausages

1. Slice the cabbage, onion and green pepper. Skin and quarter the tomatoes. Halve the mushrooms keeping just a few whole ones for the top of the dish.
2. Turn the cabbage, onion and green pepper in hot butter in a flameproof dish. Season with lemon juice, salt and paprika then cover and cook over a low heat.
3. After 10 minutes, add the tomatoes and halved mushrooms, sprinkle with salt and continue cooking for 5 minutes.
4. Arrange the Frankfurter sausages on the top of the dish like the spokes of a wheel. Put the whole mushrooms in between. Baste with juices from the dish, cover and cook for 10 minutes.
5. Serve straight from the flameproof dish.

Scotch Mushrooms

For 4

4 large cup mushrooms
1 oz butter
1–1½ lb sausage-meat

1 egg
breadcrumbs
fat for deep frying

1. Cook the mushrooms in hot butter for 4 minutes. Season with salt and pepper.
2. Cover each mushroom with sausage-meat, coat in beaten egg and breadcrumbs.
3. Fry in hot deep fat until golden.
4. Drain on kitchen paper. Serve hot with chips or cold with a salad.

Savoury Egg Flan

For 4

6–8 oz shortcrust pastry	lemon juice
4 oz liver sausage	4 large eggs
½ lb mushrooms	paprika

1. Line an 8-inch flan case with the pastry and bake 'blind' in oven 375 degrees F, mark 5.
2. Remove skin and fat from the liver sausage and cut into thin slices.
3. Slice mushrooms finely and turn in hot butter; season with salt, pepper and lemon juice and cook for 4 minutes.
4. Arrange the liver sausage slices in the flan case, cover with the mushrooms.
5. Break the eggs on top of the mushrooms. Sprinkle with salt and paprika.
6. Bake in oven for 10–15 minutes or until eggs are cooked to your liking.

Egg and Mushroom Curry

For 4

12 oz mushrooms	1 stock cube
1½ oz dripping	¾ pint water
1 level tablespoon flour	1 bay leaf
1 level tablespoon curry powder	4 hard-boiled eggs
1 level tablespoon tomato paste	6–8 oz rice

1. Slice mushrooms, sprinkle with salt, turn in hot dripping for 2 minutes. Remove from the pan.
2. Stir flour into remaining fat in pan. Add curry powder, tomato paste, stock cube and water. Stir together over a moderate heat until the sauce slightly thickens.
3. Put the bay leaf, eggs and mushrooms into the sauce. Cover and simmer for 10 minutes.
4. Cook the rice in boiling salted water until tender; drain well.
5. Put the rice onto a hot serving dish and cover with the egg and mushroom curry.

Cheese and Egg Flan

For 4

½ lb shortcrust pastry *4 eggs (poached)*
6 oz mushrooms (sliced) *½ pint thick cheese sauce*
1 oz butter *2 oz cheese (grated)*

1. Roll out the pastry and line a flan case. Bake 'blind' in oven 400 degrees F, mark 6.
2. Melt the butter in a pan and lightly fry the mushrooms; season with salt and pepper. Turn the mushrooms into the flan case.
3. Arrange the eggs on top of the mushrooms and coat with cheese sauce.
4. Top with grated cheese and finish under a hot grill.

Cheese Fritters

For 3

2 oz mushrooms (chopped) *1 large potato (raw, peeled)*
2 oz cheese (grated) *1 egg*
1 oz self-raising flour *fat for frying*
¼ teaspoon mustard

1. Cook the mushrooms in hot fat until the liquid has evaporated.

2. Put cheese, flour, mustard, mushrooms and $\frac{1}{2}$ teaspoon salt, $\frac{1}{4}$ teaspoon pepper into a bowl.

3. Shred the potato onto a plate and drain off any liquid. Put potato into the bowl and mix with the other ingredients.

4. Bind mixture with beaten egg.

5. Heat a little fat in a frying pan and put spoonsful of the mixture into the pan.

6. When golden turn the fritters, press gently with a fish slice and finish cooking slowly.

Cheese and Bacon Curls

For 4

$\frac{3}{4}$ *lb onions*
2 oz butter
$\frac{3}{4}$ *lb button mushrooms*
4 hard-boiled eggs
6 oz cheese (grated)

$\frac{3}{4}$ *pint coating white sauce*
6–8 oz streaky bacon
* rashers*
parsley (chopped)

1. Cut onions into rings and poach in a pan of boiling salted water. When tender, drain and put into an ovenproof dish.

2. Heat the butter in a shallow pan, add the mushrooms, whole, season with salt and pepper and cook for 4 minutes.

3. Halve the eggs; put mushrooms and eggs into the dish.

4. Put 4 oz cheese into the white sauce; stir over a moderate heat, check seasoning, then pour into the dish.

5. Top the dish with the remaining cheese and brown under a hot grill.

6. In the meantime, roll the bacon rashers, thread onto a skewer and grill until cooked throughout.

7. Arrange the bacon curls on top of the dish. Garnish with parsley.

Crusty Cheese Bake

For 4

6 slices bread (buttered)
½ lb mushrooms (sliced)
4 oz chopped ham (diced)
5 oz cheese (grated)

2 eggs
½ teaspoon dry mustard
½ pint milk

1. Cut each slice of bread into 4 triangles. Put one third of the bread into a buttered ovenproof dish.
2. Add half the mushrooms and ham and 2 oz cheese. Sprinkle with salt and pepper.
3. Add another third of bread triangles.
4. Use the remaining mushrooms and ham and another 2 oz cheese. Season.
5. Top the dish with bread and remaining cheese.
6. Beat the eggs with the mustard and milk. Pour into the dish.
7. Bake in oven 350 degrees F, mark 4 for about 45 minutes.

Cauliflower Crisp

For 4

1 cauliflower
6 oz bacon (chopped)
8 oz mushrooms (sliced)
2 oz butter

¾ pint cheese sauce
2 oz cheese (grated)
2 tablespoons breadcrumbs
   (browned)

1. Clean and trim the cauliflower; cook in boiling salted water until just tender; drain well.
2. Sauté the bacon and mushrooms in hot butter for 4 minutes.
3. Divide the cauliflower between 4 individual ovenproof dishes; cover with bacon and mushroom mixture.
4. Pour over the cheese sauce, then sprinkle with cheese and breadcrumbs. Brown under a hot grill. Garnish with parsley.

Salads, Vegetables and Preserves

THIS SECTION includes a variety of accompanying dishes, hot and cold, cooked and raw.

Fresh vegetables are an essential part of a balanced diet to keep the body healthy. Mushrooms contain nutrients in the form of protein, minerals and vitamins and have no fat or carbohydrate which gives them a low calorific value—particularly attractive to slimmers.

Alpine Ray

For 4

4 oz Gruyère cheese	*12 oz cottage cheese*
½ cucumber	*3 oz sultanas*
6 oz button mushrooms	*paprika*
1 lemon	

1. Dice the Gruyère cheese and cucumber. Quarter the mushrooms.
2. Peel the lemon, remove as much pith and skin as possible. Cut the segments into quarters.
3. Mix all the ingredients with the cottage cheese.
4. Season with salt and paprika pepper to taste. Serve well chilled.

Blue Cheese and Watercress Salad

For 6

½ lb blue cheese
6 spring onions
2 sticks celery
6 oz button mushrooms
paprika
2 bunches watercress (crisp
and chilled)

1 tablespoon olive oil
1 tablespoon lemon juice
1 tablespoon nuts (finely
chopped, toasted)

1. Cut the cheese into small cubes. Slice the spring onions. Chop the celery. Slice the mushrooms. Mix all these ingredients together and sprinkle with paprika.
2. Strip the leaves from the stems of the watercress. Turn the leaves in a mixture of oil and lemon juice.
3. Sprinkle the watercress with toasted nuts, toss lightly and turn into a bowl.
4. Spoon the blue cheese mixture into the centre and sprinkle with paprika.

Cranberry Salad

For 4

½ lb button mushrooms
4 oz tiny onions
3 sticks celery (chopped)
3 small carrots (finely
sliced)
¼ pint good Consommé

1 dessertspoon cranberry
jelly
black pepper
bay leaf
1 tablespoon chives
(chopped)
chicory

1. Put the mushrooms, onion, celery and carrot into a pan.
2. Pour in the Consommé and add the cranberry jelly.
3. Season with salt, freshly ground black pepper and bay leaf.

Mushrooms à la Grecque (page 43).

4. Cook uncovered for about 20 minutes, stirring occasionally.
5. Turn into a glass dish and allow to become cold. Sprinkle with chopped chives and decorate the dish with chicory.

Crazy Capers

For 6

2 tablespoons capers
1 teaspoon Worcestershire
    sauce
½ teaspoon paprika
1 tablespoon chives
    (chopped)

2 5 oz cartons soured cream
½ lb button mushrooms
1 lb tomatoes
watercress

1. Blend the capers, Worcestershire sauce, paprika and chives with the soured cream. Add salt to taste.
2. Slice the mushrooms and stir into the sauce.
3. Halve the tomatoes and make an arrangement with these in the centre of a dish.
4. Set the mushroom and caper salad around the tomatoes. Garnish with sprigs of watercress.

Curried Cream Salad

For 4–6

2 5 oz cartons soured cream
1 teaspoon curry powder
1 teaspoon mango chutney
    sauce

lemon juice
½ lb button mushrooms
    (sliced)
6 oz ham (diced)

1. Turn the soured cream into a bowl and blend in the curry powder and chutney sauce. Add salt and pepper and lemon juice to taste.
2. Stir in the mushrooms and most of the ham.

Green-collared Trout (page 109).

3. Arrange in a dish garnished with the remaining ham and sprinkled with a little curry powder.

Eugene's Turkey Salad

For 4

1 tablespoon olive oil	*2 sticks celery*
6 oz mushrooms (sliced)	*1 oz walnuts*
lemon juice	*6 oz cold turkey*
1 oz shredded almonds	*mayonnaise*
1 eating apple	*lettuce*

1. Heat the oil in a pan, add the mushrooms; sprinkle with lemon juice, salt and pepper. Cook for 4 minutes.
2. Turn the mushrooms onto a plate and leave until cold.
3. Turn the almonds in the pan, lightly sprinkled with salt, and cook until golden. Put aside to cool.
4. Core and chop the apple. Chop the celery, walnuts and turkey.
5. Mix all the above ingredients together with the mushrooms and almonds.
6. Moisten with mayonnaise and turn into a salad dish lined with lettuce.

French Mushroom Salad

For 4–6

½ lb button mushrooms	*1 lettuce*
4 tablespoons vegetable oil	*1 tablespoon capers*
3 tablespoons vinegar	*1 tablespoon pimento*
½ teaspoon French mustard	*(minced)*
pinch cayenne	*2 hard-boiled eggs*

1. Slice the mushrooms.
2. Mix oil, vinegar, mustard and cayenne together with a good pinch of salt. For the best result, shake in a screw-top jar.
3. Pour the dressing over the mushrooms and leave to stand in a

refrigerator. The flavour will improve if the mushrooms can be left to stand overnight or for several hours.

4. Prepare the lettuce and arrange the leaves on a dish.

5. Strain the mushrooms from the dressing and spoon onto the centre of the dish.

6. Scatter capers and pimento over the top.

7. Use eggs, sliced or quartered to make a border round the mushroom salad.

Green Salad

For 4

> 2 dessert apples (*chopped*)
> 4 oz mushrooms (*chopped*)
> lemon juice
> 4 sticks celery
> spring onions
>
> *1 lettuce*
> *1 oz button mushrooms*
>   (*sliced*)
> *2 oz gherkins*
> *2 oz cheese* (*finely grated*)

1. Mix the apple and mushrooms, sprinkle with salt and lemon juice.

2. Add celery, finely chopped, and a few onions, also chopped.

3. Arrange this mixture on a bed of lettuce.

4. Decorate the dish with spring onions, mushrooms and gherkins; pile the cheese in the centre.

Golden Chicken Salad

For 4

> *1 large orange*
> *1–2 teaspoons lemon juice*
> *2 tablespoons sultanas*
> *1 oz blanched almonds*
>
> $\frac{3}{4}$ *lb chicken* (*cooked*)
> *6 oz button mushrooms*
> *3 sticks celery*
> *1 small bunch watercress*

1. Finely grate the orange skin. Squeeze the orange juice and mix these with the lemon juice. Soak the sultanas and almonds in the fruit juices for 1 hour.

2. Chop the chicken and finely slice the mushrooms. Finely chop the celery and watercress. Mix all these ingredients together.
3. Turn the salad into a dish. Pour over the fruit juice and arrange the almonds and sultanas on top of the dish.
4. Garnish with fine twists of orange and lemon peel.

Golden Rain

For 4

½ lb mushrooms
½ cucumber
1 large tin Mexicorn

½ bottle Sweet and Sour
 dressing
4 hard-boiled eggs

1. Finely slice mushrooms, dice cucumber and mix with drained Mexicorn.
2. Season and turn in the dressing. Leave to stand in a cool place for 30 minutes.
3. Serve on a salad dish, bordered with slices of hard-boiled egg.

Gruyère Cheese Salad

For 6

6 oz Gruyère cheese
3 hard-boiled eggs
6 oz button mushrooms
1 5 oz carton soured cream
4 tablespoons mayonnaise

½ teaspoon mustard powder
½ teaspoon creamed horse-
 radish
onion salt
1 lettuce

1. Cut the cheese into thin sticks.
2. Slice one hard-boiled egg; put aside a few rings of egg for garnish, then mix the rest with the other eggs and chop coarsely.
3. Chop the mushrooms.
4. Mix the soured cream and mayonnaise together. Stir in the mustard and horseradish. Season with onion salt and white pepper.

5. Mix the cheese, egg and mushrooms with the dressing.
6. Turn into a salad bowl lined with lettuce leaves.
7. Garnish with rings of egg.

Ham Salad Rolls

For 4

8 slices ham	1 teaspoon mint (chopped)
4 oz liver pâté	1 teaspoon lemon juice
1 dessert apple	2 tablespoons mayonnaise
4 oz mushrooms	1 oz walnuts (chopped)
4 sticks celery	green salad

1. Spread the slices of ham with pâté.
2. Peel, core and chop the apple. Chop mushrooms and celery.
3. Stir mint and lemon juice into the mayonnaise.
4. Mix apple, mushrooms, celery and walnuts with the dressing. Season with salt and pepper.
5. Cover the slices of ham with the mixture and roll up each slice. Chill until ready to serve.
6. Arrange on a bed of green salad.

Macaroni and Salmon Salad

For 4–6

4 oz egg macaroni shells	1 tablespoon onion (chopped)
7½ oz tin salmon (flaked)	6 tablespoons salad dressing
4 oz cooked peas	of your choice
2 oz mushrooms (sliced)	lettuce
2 celery stalks (diced)	1 hard-boiled egg (sliced)
2 tablespoons sweet pickle	cucumber (sliced)

1. Cook the macaroni shells according to the instructions on the packet. Drain, rinse with cold water, drain again and chill.
2. Mix the shells, salmon, peas, mushrooms, celery, pickle and onion together. Toss in salad dressing.

3. Serve on a bed of lettuce and garnish with sliced egg and cucumber.

Mushroom and Almond Vinaigrette

For 4

6 oz white cabbage	black pepper
6 oz mushrooms	1 oz blanched almonds
4 tablespoons oil	1 tablespoon gherkin
3 tablespoons wine vinegar	(chopped)
½ teaspoon French mustard	

1. Remove the stalks from the cabbage and shred it very finely.
2. Slice the mushrooms finely and put into a bowl with the cabbage.
3. Mix the oil, vinegar and mustard with salt and black pepper in a screw-top jar and shake well.
4. Pour over the cabbage and mushrooms and mix well. Cover and leave to stand in a cool place, preferably overnight.
5. When ready to serve, put the mushroom and cabbage into a salad dish and scatter chopped almonds and gherkins over the top.

Mushroom and Cottage Cheese Salad

For 4–6

1 lb cottage cheese	1 lettuce (or ½ lb fresh
cayenne pepper	spinach)
1 teaspoon onion (grated)	4 hard-boiled eggs
½ teaspoon mustard	1 tablespoon chives (chopped)
½ lb button mushrooms	
(sliced)	

1. Season the cottage cheese with salt, cayenne, onion and mustard.
2. Add the mushrooms and stir together.
3. Set on a dish lined with chopped lettuce or spinach.
4. Top with hard-boiled eggs and sprinkle with chopped chives.

Pink Pearls

For 4

12 oz cottage cheese
1 teaspoon paprika
½ teaspoon Worcestershire
   sauce
few drops Tabasco sauce

½ lb small button mush-
   rooms (whole or
   quartered)
1–2 heads chicory
chives (chopped)

1. Stir the cottage cheese with a fork. Add paprika, Worcestershire sauce and Tabasco sauce, salt and pepper.
2. Chill the mixture for at least 30 minutes.
3. When ready to serve, stir the mushrooms with the mixture
and turn into a dish edged with chicory.
4. Sprinkle a little paprika or chopped chives over the dish.

Potato 'Hedgehog' Salad

For 6–8

1¼ lb creamed potato (cold)
3 tablespoons double cream
4 tablespoons mayonnaise
½ teaspoon Worcestershire
   sauce
½ lb cup mushrooms
2 tablespoons gherkins
   (chopped)

1 tablespoon capers
2 tablespoons celery (diced)
3 tablespoons chives
   (chopped)
2–3 whole gherkins
2–3 whole mushrooms

1. Beat the potatoes with the cream, mayonnaise and Worcestershire sauce until fluffy. Season well with salt and pepper.
2. Chop the mushrooms, mix half into the potato.
3. Stir in chopped gherkins, capers and celery and turn onto a
flat dish. Shape the potato mixture to that of a hedgehog's body,
scatter the chives as the body spikes, and use the gherkins and
mushrooms for the face.
4. Put the remaining chopped mushrooms round the dish.

Salad Tartare

For 4

> *1 tablespoon gherkins*
> *(chopped)*
> *1 tablespoon capers (chopped)*
> *1 teaspoon onion (grated)*
> *⅓ pint mayonnaise*
>
> *lemon juice*
> *½ lb button mushrooms*
> *(sliced)*
> *cucumber slices*

1. Mix the gherkins, capers and onion with the mayonnaise. Season with salt and pepper. Add lemon juice to taste.
2. Stir the mushrooms and dressing together and chill.
3. Turn the mushroom mixture into a dish and decorate with slices of cucumber.

Shrimp and Cucumber Salad

For 4

> *4 oz button mushrooms*
> *2 sticks celery*
> *½ lb shrimps (peeled)*
> *cucumber*
> *3 hard-boiled eggs*
>
> *4 tablespoons mayonnaise*
> *(thinned with a little*
> *cream)*
> *paprika*

1. Dice the mushrooms and celery. Mix with the shrimps.
2. Arrange slices of cucumber on a flat dish.
3. Slice the hard-boiled eggs and make a pattern like the spokes of a wheel on top of the cucumber.
4. Spoon the shrimp mixture in between the egg.
5. Lightly coat each section of shrimps with mayonnaise.
6. Garnish with paprika.

Sour Cream Coleslaw

For 4

1 small clove garlic
½ teaspoon paprika
1 5 oz carton soured cream
lemon juice
¾ lb firm white cabbage

4 oz button mushrooms
1 oz blanched almonds
1 dessertspoon chives
(chopped)

1. Crush the garlic. Blend garlic and paprika into the cream.
2. Season with a little salt and lemon juice.
3. Wash the cabbage, trim away hard stalk and shred the cabbage very finely.
4. Finely slice the mushrooms and shred the almonds.
5. Turn the cabbage and mushrooms in the dressing until evenly coated.
6. Spoon into a salad dish and scatter nuts and chives over the top.

Sunset Salad

For 4

4 tablespoons cider vinegar
½ teaspoon Worcestershire
   sauce
½ teaspoon mustard
¾ lb tomatoes (skinned)

10 spring onions
½ cucumber
4 oz mushrooms
parsley (chopped)

1. Blend together vinegar, Worcestershire sauce and mustard.
2. Slice tomatoes, onions, cucumber and mushrooms.
3. Turn the vegetables in the dressing.
4. Chill mixture for 1 hour.
5. Serve in a glass dish. Sprinkle with chopped parsley.

Sweet Salad with Chicken

For 4

2 oz long grain rice
1 oz blanched almonds
2 oz butter
1 tablespoon lemon juice
½ lb mushrooms
2 tablespoons pineapple
  (chopped)

2 teaspoons mango chutney
½ teaspoon curry powder
4 portions chicken (cooked)
bunch watercress

1. Cook the rice in boiling salted water. When tender, wash, drain well and leave aside until cold.
2. Fry the almonds in hot butter until golden; remove from the pan and drain on kitchen paper.
3. Add lemon juice and sliced mushrooms to the pan, cook over a fierce heat for 1 minute; remove from pan and set aside until cold.
4. Mix pineapple, almonds, mushrooms and chopped mango with rice.
5. Sprinkle with curry powder, salt and pepper and stir thoroughly.
6. Turn onto the centre of a dish and arrange the chicken round the edge.
7. Garnish with watercress.

Buttered Mushrooms

For 4

1 lb mushrooms
3 oz butter
black pepper

1 lemon
chives (chopped)

1. Slice the mushrooms.
2. Heat the butter in a pan or flameproof dish, add the mush-

rooms. Season with salt, black pepper and lemon juice.

3. Cover and simmer for about 10 minutes.

4. Serve garnished with slices of lemon and chopped chives.

Burgundy Special

For 4

1 lb mushrooms	*3 oz butter*
1 onion	*1 rounded teaspoon flour*
2 oz green pepper	*1 wineglass Red Burgundy*
1 clove garlic	

1. Quarter the mushrooms. Finely slice onion and green pepper. Crush garlic with a little salt.

2. Heat the butter in a shallow pan, add garlic and after a few moments, add the onion and pepper. Simmer gently until tender.

3. Add the mushrooms, sprinkle with salt and pepper, cover and cook for 4 minutes.

4. Stir in the flour, then add the wine. Cook over a low heat until the mushrooms are coated in a creamy red wine sauce.

5. Serve as a special vegetable at a dinner party; or as a filling for pastry or bread cases or simply on hot buttered toast.

Eastern Mushrooms

For 4

3 oz butter	*1 tablespoon lemon juice*
1 lb mushrooms (sliced)	*1 tablespoon Soy sauce*
black pepper	*1 tablespoon parsley*
2 oz split almonds	*(chopped)*

1. Heat the butter in a frying pan. Season with salt and freshly ground black pepper and cook for 3 minutes.

2. Add the almonds, lemon juice, Soy sauce and parsley. Turn over a fierce heat for 2 minutes.
3. Turn into a hot serving dish.

This dish makes an excellent accompaniment to rice dishes.

Mixed Vegetable Bake

For 4

4 courgettes	*6 oz button mushrooms*
1 aubergine	*⅛ pint dry cider*
4 sticks celery	*1 tin tomato sauce*
4 oz tiny onions	

1. Slice the courgettes, aubergine and celery.
2. Wash the mushrooms, skin the onions and leave both whole.
3. Mix the vegetables and put into an ovenproof dish. Season well with salt and ground black pepper.
4. Pour the cider into the dish and the tomato sauce over the top of the vegetables.
5. Cover the dish and cook in oven 375 degrees F, mark 5 for 45 minutes.

Mushrooms and Carrots

For 6

2 oz butter	*1 tablespoon chives (chopped)*
2 tablespoons oil	*black pepper*
1 tablespoon parsley	*1 lb carrots*
(chopped)	*1 lb mushrooms (sliced)*

1. Heat the butter and oil in a large shallow pan. Add the chopped parsley and chives, season with salt and freshly ground black pepper.
2. Put the carrots (whole, if small, otherwise cut lengthwise) into

the pan, add the mushrooms and turn over a moderate heat for a minute.

3. Reduce the heat, cover the pan with a lid or foil and simmer gently for about 15 minutes.

4. Turn ingredients into a hot serving dish.

Mushroom Crumble

For 4

1 lb mushrooms
4 tablespoons oil
fine breadcrumbs

1 clove garlic
1 tablespoon parsley
(chopped)

1. Heat the oil in a large frying pan, add the whole mushrooms, season with salt and freshly ground black pepper; cover and cook for about 4 minutes.

2. Lift the mushrooms out of the pan with a draining spoon and put into a hot serving dish.

3. Toss the breadcrumbs and finely crushed garlic with the rest of the oil in the pan. Cook gently until golden.

4. Stir in the parsley and scatter the mixture over the mushrooms.

Mushroom Medley

For 3–4

1 oz butter
1 onion (chopped)
¾ lb mushrooms (sliced)
½ pint dry cider

pinch thyme
parsley (chopped)
lemon

1. Heat the butter in a pan; add onion and simmer until soft.

2. Add mushrooms, cider, salt, pepper and a pinch of thyme to the pan.

3. Cover with a well-fitting lid and simmer for 10 minutes.

4. Strain the mushrooms into a hot serving dish.

5. Reduce the liquid in the pan over a fierce heat for 2 minutes, then pour over the mushrooms.

6. Sprinkle with chopped parsley and garnish with slices of lemon.

Mushrooms in Foil

For 4

    1 lb open or cup mush-   *salt and pepper*
    rooms

1. Take a large sheet of cooking foil and place it flat on the table.

2. Clean the mushrooms and put these in the centre of the foil. Sprinkle well with salt and pepper.

3. Seal the foil and put the parcel into oven 400 degrees F, mark 6 for about 15 minutes.

4. Serve as a vegetable.

5. Alternatively, use the mushrooms for garnishing other dishes.

This dish contains very few Calories and can be eaten in quantity by those on a slimming diet. Use a selection of seasonings to give variety.

Mushrooms in Milk

For 3–4

    1½ oz butter   *½ pint milk*
    ¾ lb mushrooms   *bay leaf*
    black pepper   *parsley (chopped)*

1. Heat the butter in a pan. Add the mushrooms, sprinkle with salt and freshly ground black pepper and cook for a minute.

2. Pour in enough milk to almost cover the mushrooms. Add a bay leaf (if liked).

3. Cover the pan with a well-fitting lid and simmer the mushrooms very gently for about 15 minutes or until the mushrooms are tender.
4. Strain off the milk. Put the mushrooms into a dish and sprinkle with a little parsley.
5. Alternatively, thicken the milk with a little cornflour and pour this over the mushrooms.

Royal Mushrooms

For 4–6

2 oz butter	*2 tablespoons sherry*
1 lb button mushrooms	*¾ pint tomato pulp*
2 tablespoons onion (minced)	*4 oz cream cheese*
black pepper	*parsley (chopped)*
pinch tarragon	

1. Heat the butter in a pan, add the mushrooms, whole or quartered, and the minced onion. Sprinkle with salt and freshly ground black pepper. Cook for 2 minutes.
2. Scatter the tarragon over the vegetables and pour in the sherry.
3. Increase the heat, pour in the tomato pulp then season and cook until tomato has reduced by half.
4. Stir in the cream cheese over the heat.
5. Turn into a hot serving dish. Sprinkle with parsley.

Mushroom Ketchup

10 lb fresh open mushrooms	*¼ teaspoon cayenne pepper*
½ lb cooking salt	*¼ teaspoon ground ginger*
	¼ teaspoon allspice

1. Brush off any dirt from the mushrooms but do not wet them.
2. Break the mushrooms into small pieces and put into a large bowl. Sprinkle each layer with a generous amount of salt and top the bowl with salt.
3. Leave to stand in a cool place for 48 hours, stirring with a wooden spoon at frequent intervals.
4. Turn into a large enamel pan and simmer for about 20 minutes.
5. Strain the liquor, measure it and put into a clean pan.
6. Add the spices according to the measure.
7. Boil the ketchup until it has reduced by half.
8. Leave to cool. When completely cold put into clean dry bottles, seal and label.

A little Port, Madeira or Brandy may be added at the end of cooking.

Pickled Mushrooms

$1\frac{1}{2}$ lb small button mush- $\frac{1}{2}$ pint vinegar
    rooms   6 peppercorns
1 tablespoon salt

1. Wash the mushrooms thoroughly. Dry on kitchen paper.
2. Put into a pan, sprinkling each layer of mushrooms with salt.
3. Cover the pan with a well-fitting lid and simmer very gently until the mushrooms are tender but not soft.
4. Boil the vinegar with the peppercorns in another pan. Leave to cool.
5. Fill sterilized jars with the mushrooms. Add 1 tablespoon of the liquor to each jar then fill the jar with cold boiled vinegar.
6. Seal and label the jars.

To allow the vinegar to penetrate the mushrooms, store for 14 days before using. When cooked, approximately $\frac{3}{4}$ lb raw mushrooms will fill 1 lb jam jar.

Mushroom and Apple Chutney

Yield: approx. 2 lb.

2 pints white vinegar	4 oz red pepper
1 lb cooking apples	¾ lb green tomatoes
1 medium onion	¾ lb brown sugar
1 lb mushrooms	2 cloves garlic

1. Pour the vinegar into a large pan and bring to the boil.
2. Peel, core and chop the apples. Put into the pan and simmer over a low heat.
3. Chop the onion, mushroom and pepper and add these to the pan.
4. Chop the tomatoes, add these to the pan together with the sugar.
5. Crush the garlic, put it into a muslin and place it in the pan.
6. Simmer the mixture until it becomes a thick consistency with almost no liquid. Stir the mixture at intervals.
7. Remove the garlic. Turn the chutney into sterilized jars and seal at once.
8. Label and store.

Red Tomato Chutney

Yield: approx. 3 lb.

5 lb ripe tomatoes	2½ pints malt vinegar
3 onions (thinly sliced)	2 tablespoons salt
3 green peppers (thinly sliced)	2 lemons (grated rind and juice)
2 lb mushrooms (thinly sliced)	1 teaspoon ground mixed spice

1. Skin and quarter the tomatoes. Remove most of the seeds and put the flesh and juice into a large pan.
2. Add all the other ingredients and boil gently for at least 1 hour until the chutney is a thick consistency.
3. Put into sterilized jars. Seal and label.

Home Entertaining

DISHES FOR dinner parties, buffet parties, cocktail parties and informal entertaining.

Choose dishes which do not require a lot of personal supervision and try them at least once before you serve it to guests. You will then be more confident of yourself and the dish.

Well cooked simple dishes are always more acceptable than badly cooked exotic dishes. Don't spend more than you can really afford on expensive foods; make the best of inexpensive foods, using a touch of luxury to turn them into something special.

Fresh Haddock Cutlets in Cider

For 4

> *4 fresh haddock cutlets*
> *½ lb cup mushrooms*
> *1 teaspoon onion (grated)*
> *1½ oz butter*
> *3 oz white grapes*

> *2 tablespoons dried bread-*
> *crumbs*
> *½ pint dry cider*
> *2 tomatoes (sliced)*

1. Place the fish cutlets in an ovenproof dish.
2. Chop the mushrooms; turn mushrooms and onion in hot butter until tender. Season with salt and pepper.
3. Quarter the grapes and remove the pips. Put the grapes and breadcrumbs into the pan and mix with the mushrooms and onion.

4. Top each cutlet with the mixture. Pour the cider round the fish.

5. Cover the dish with a lid or foil and bake in oven 375 degrees F, mark 5 for about 30 minutes.

6. Put the fish onto a serving dish; reduce the cider stock by half in a pan over a fierce heat, then pour round the fish. Garnish with slices of tomato.

Halibut Lucinda

For 4

1 egg
1½ lb creamed potatoes
4 halibut steaks
black pepper
lemon juice
2 oz butter
4 oz button mushrooms (sliced)

1 oz flour
¼ pint dry white wine
¼ pint milk
2 tablespoons double cream
½ lb white grapes (skinned and seeded)
paprika
parsley

1. Beat the egg into the potato over a moderate heat. Pipe the potato round the edge of an ovenproof dish.

2. Sprinkle the fish with salt, pepper and lemon juice and put into the dish.

3. Melt the butter in a pan, add the mushrooms, season and cook for 3 minutes.

4. Stir in the flour and gradually add the wine and milk. Bring to the boil and simmer for 3 minutes.

5. Stir in the cream, grapes and paprika to taste. Simmer gently for a minute.

6. Pour the sauce over the fish. Cook in oven 350 degrees F, mark 4 for about 35 minutes.

7. Garnish with paprika and parsley.

Green Collared Trout

For 4

4 trout
4 open mushrooms
1¼ lb cup mushrooms
2 medium onions

1 wine glass dry white wine
1 small green pepper
1 lemon

1. Put the fish and four whole mushrooms (for garnish) into a shallow ovenproof dish. Pour over the wine and season with salt and pepper. Cover and poach in oven 375 degrees F, mark 5 for about 25 minutes.
2. Mince mushrooms, onion and half the green pepper.
3. Strain wine from the fish into a shallow pan; add mushrooms, onion and green pepper. Season with salt, pepper and lemon juice and cook over a moderate heat until all the liquid has evaporated.
4. Skin the fish (if liked).
5. Put the mushroom mixture onto a hot serving dish. Arrange the fish on top.
6. Put a collar of green pepper on each fish and garnish the dish with slices of lemon and whole mushrooms.

Plaice Pockets

For 4

4 whole plaice
2 oz butter
10 oz mushrooms
3 teaspoons onion (grated)

1 tablespoon chives (chopped)
1 lemon
⅓ pint fish stock

1. Lay fish, black skin uppermost, on a board, cut straight down the backbone with a sharp knife. Slip the knife under the flesh on each side of the cut, so forming a pocket.
2. Heat butter in a pan, add sliced mushrooms and onion, chopped chives, a squeeze of lemon juice, salt and pepper. Cook for 3 minutes.

3. Fill fish pockets with mixture.

4. Place in an ovenproof dish, pour in the stock and sprinkle with salt.

5. Cover and cook in oven 350 degrees F, mark 4 for about 25 minutes.

6. Serve with lemon slices and chives.

Stuffed Plaice Fillets

For 4

1 oz butter
1 tablespoon onion (chopped)
6 oz mushrooms (chopped)
*1 heaped teaspoon parsley
  (chopped)*
2 tablespoons breadcrumbs

8 small plaice fillets
¾ pint Bechamel sauce
paprika
*whole grilled mushrooms for
  garnish*

1. Heat the butter in a pan and add the chopped ingredients. Simmer gently until tender. Season with salt and pepper and bind together with breadcrumbs.

2. Put the fillets, skin-side uppermost, onto a board and divide the mixture evenly between the fillets. Roll up fillets and place in a buttered ovenproof dish.

3. Pour over the sauce, cover and bake in oven 400 degrees F, mark 6 for about 25 minutes.

4. Garnish with paprika and grilled mushrooms.

Cutlet Cream

For 4

4 cutlets white fish
2½ oz butter
¼ pint milk
½ oz flour
5 oz carton soured cream

Tabasco sauce
pinch of Basil
1 tablespoon chives (chopped)
4 tomatoes (fried)

1. Poach the fish in 1 oz butter and ¼ pint milk. Season with salt and pepper, cover and cook until tender.
2. Heat 1½ oz butter in a shallow pan, add onion and cook gently until soft but not browned.
3. Add sliced mushrooms to the onions, season and cook for 3 minutes.
4. Sprinkle the flour into the pan, stir well and cook for a moment. Pour in the soured cream, add a dash of Tabasco sauce and a pinch of Basil.
5. Heat gently until the sauce thickens. Add a little of the stock from the fish pan to give a smooth coating sauce.
6. Arrange the cutlets on a hot serving dish and pour over the sauce.
7. Garnish with chopped chives and fried tomato halves.

Cold Shellfish Risotto

For 4

6 oz long grain rice
1 pint fresh prawns
6 oz button mushrooms
½ lb crabmeat
1 dozen prepared mussels
   (sliced)

½ pint double cream
1 tablespoon mayonnaise
paprika
1 teaspoon onion (grated)
horseradish (grated)
1 tablespoon chives
   (chopped)

1. Boil the rice in salted water until just soft, then rinse well in cold water. Drain and allow to become cold.
2. Peel prawns and slice mushrooms.
3. Mix crabmeat, prawns, mussels and mushrooms with the rice.
4. Whip the cream and stir in the mayonnaise. Add salt, paprika, onion and grated horseradish to taste.
5. Turn the rice and fish mixture into a bowl. Pour over the sauce and top with finely chopped chives.

Curried Mussels and Mushrooms

For 4

½ lb long grain rice
2 quarts fresh mussels
½ pint white wine (or dry cider)
2 bay leaves
1 small onion

1½ oz butter
½ lb mushrooms (quartered)
½ oz flour
1 level dessertspoon curry powder

1. Boil the rice in salted water until tender. Drain well.
2. Clean the mussels thoroughly and put into a large pan. Add wine, bay leaves and sliced onion. Cover tightly and cook until the mussels have opened; about 3–4 minutes.
3. Keep the stock; remove the mussels from the shells.
4. Heat butter in a pan, add mushrooms, sprinkle with salt and cook for 4 minutes. Remove from the pan.
5. Add flour and curry powder to the fat in the pan and stir well. Blend in the wine stock and bring to the boil.
6. Put the mussels and mushrooms into the sauce and simmer for 5 minutes.
7. Serve on a bed of rice edged with wedges of hard-boiled egg and tomato.

Scallops in Wine

For 4

12 oz puff pastry
1 beaten egg
¾ lb button mushrooms
12 little scallops
1 wineglass dry white wine
1 bay leaf

½ pint thick Bechamel sauce
onion salt
black pepper
1 egg yolk
parsley

1. Roll out the pastry to a circular shape to make one large vol-au-vent case. Mark an inner circle for the 'lid'. Brush the top with beaten egg and bake in oven 400 degrees F, mark 6 for about 25 minutes.

2. When the case is crisp, remove the 'lid' and take out the soft centre pastry. Return the case to the oven for a few more minutes.

3. Quarter the mushrooms. Put mushrooms and scallops into a pan with the wine. Add bay leaf, salt and pepper and simmer until tender.

4. Stir in the Bechamel sauce. Season with onion salt and freshly ground black pepper.

5. Finally stir in the egg yolk and heat very gently.

6. Fill the pastry case with the mixture. Top with the pastry lid and garnish with sprigs of parsley.

Beef in Beer

For 4

1½ lb topside of beef
(without added fat)
1 onion (sliced)
6 peppercorns
1 bay leaf
½ teaspoon thyme
1 teaspoon mustard

1 pint light ale
black pepper
¾ lb mushrooms
½ lb courgettes
oil
cornflour

1. Cut the meat into four equal slices.

2. Put the onion, peppercorns, bay leaf, thyme and mustard into a large bowl. Pour in the beer and season with salt and black pepper. Mix well.

3. Put the meat into the marinade. Cover and leave to stand for 12 hours.

4. Slice mushrooms and courgettes and toss in a little hot oil. Turn into a casserole dish.

5. Put the meat on top of the vegetables and pour over the beer and seasonings.

6. Cover with a lid and cook in oven 400 degrees F, mark 6 for about 1 hour or until meat is tender.

7. Arrange the meat and vegetables on a hot serving dish; thicken the strained stock with cornflour and pour over.

Beef and Mushroom Goulash

For 4

1¼ lb stewing steak	1 teaspoon marjoram
¾ lb onions	2 oz butter
½ lb mushrooms	1 tablespoon paprika
1 green pepper	1 15 oz tin tomatoes
1 lemon	⅓ pint stock
1 clove garlic	2 tablespoons oil

1. Cut the meat into 1-inch cubes. Slice onion, mushrooms, and finely slice the green pepper.

2. Grate the rind of the lemon; crush the garlic with a little salt. Mix lemon rind and garlic with marjoram.

3. Heat the butter in a large pan and add the prepared seasonings. Put the onion into the pan and cook until a golden colour. Add paprika and continue stirring over the heat.

4. Put the meat, tomatoes, juice of ½ lemon and stock into the pan and stir well; cover with a lid and simmer gently for 1½–2 hours until meat is tender.

5. Heat the oil in a shallow pan, cook the green pepper gently. After 2–3 minutes add the sliced mushrooms, season with salt and black pepper and cook until tender.

6. Serve the goulash in a hot dish and top with green peppers and mushrooms.

Beef Fiddlesticks

For 4

½ *lb long grain rice*	¾ *oz flour*
2 tablespoons red and green	½ *pint stock*
peppers (dried)	*1 tablespoon lemon juice*
1 lb frying steak	*3 tablespoons double cream*
4 oz butter	
1 tablespoon shallots	Garnish:
(chopped)	*4 oz fried mushrooms*
4 oz mushrooms (sliced)	*parsley*

1. Cook the rice and dried peppers in boiling salted water until tender, drain well.
2. Slice the steak into 'sticks', turn in hot butter until lightly browned and tender. Remove from the pan.
3. Put shallots and mushrooms into the butter; cook until soft.
4. Put the flour into the pan and stir over a low heat for 2 minutes. Add stock and lemon juice and stir until sauce thickens. Cover and simmer for 5 minutes.
5. Put the meat into the sauce, add the cream and heat through.
6. Serve the rice on a hot dish, topped with the beef sticks and garnished with fried mushrooms and parsley.

Orange Steaks

For 4

4 medium sized steaks	*3 oz seedless raisins*
8 large open mushrooms	*3 tablespoons breadcrumbs*
1 oz butter (melted)	*1 orange*
1 oz blanched almonds	

1. Brush steaks and mushrooms with butter.

2. Grill and keep warm on heatproof serving dish.

3. Lightly chop nuts and raisins, mix with crumbs and orange juice.

4. Place mushrooms on top of steaks and top each mushroom with the mixture.

5. Put dish under hot grill for a few moments until the topping is lightly browned.

6. Garnish with fine twists of orange peel.

Soho Chicken

For 6

1 chicken (approx. 3 lb)	*2 oz green pepper*
2 oz butter	*¾ pint dry white wine or*
½ lb open mushrooms	*cider*
1 large onion	*1 bay leaf*

1. Heat the butter in a large heavy pan; lightly fry the chicken on all sides and put into a casserole.

2. Put the whole mushrooms, sliced onion and finely sliced green pepper into the pan and sauté for 3 minutes. Turn into the casserole.

3. Pour the wine into the pan, stir with the pan juices over a fierce heat for 1 minute.

4. Pour wine over the chicken, season with salt and pepper and a bay leaf.

5. Cover, cook for 30 minutes in oven 375 degrees F, mark 5, then remove the lid, baste with the juices from the dish and continue cooking uncovered for a further 45 minutes, or until the meat is tender.

6. Serve on a hot carving dish with wine stock gravy served in a gravy boat.

Chicken à la Dino

For 4

3 oz butter
2 tablespoons parsley
 (chopped)
black pepper
4 tablespoons onion (chopped)
½ lb mushrooms (sliced)

4 chicken breasts (fresh and
 skinned)
1 sherry glass medium dry
 sherry
½ pint double cream
paprika

1. Heat the butter in a pan, add the parsley and sprinkle with salt and freshly ground black pepper.
2. Put the onion and mushrooms into the pan and cook until tender.
3. Season the chicken breasts and put into the pan.
4. Cook until the chicken bone rises when the meat is cooked.
5. Pour in the sherry and flame.
6. Add the cream, sprinkle with paprika and, as the cream thickens, serve onto a hot dish.

Champignons Noisettes

For 4

4 best-end cutlets of lamb
2 oz butter (melted)
4 large open mushrooms
1 eating apple

2 oz cheese (grated)
2 tomatoes
watercress

1. Ask the butcher to bone out four best-end cutlets. Tie round with string.
2. Brush the meat with melted butter and season; grill until meat is tender. Remove the string.
3. Brush the mushrooms with melted butter, season and grill for 2 minutes each side. Grill the halved tomatoes for garnish.
4. Peel and grate the apple. Mix with cheese and fill each mushroom with the mixture.

5. Put the stuffed mushrooms under the grill for a minute or two.
6. Arrange the mushrooms on top of the noisettes on a hot dish. Garnish with tomatoes and watercress.

Breast of Lamb with Pâté Stuffing

For 3

1 breast of lamb	*1 dessertspoon onion (grated)*
4 oz mushrooms	*3 oz Pâté de Foie*

1. Bone out the breast of lamb.
2. Finely chop the mushrooms and mix with the onion and pâté.
3. Spread the stuffing on the boned-side of the meat, roll up and secure with string.
4. Wrap in buttered cooking foil and bake in oven 375 degrees F, mark 5 for about 1 hour.
5. Remove the foil and serve in slices.

Garnished Lamb Chops

For 4

3 oz butter	*8 cup mushrooms*
juice of ½ lemon	*oil*
2 tablespoons parsley	*lemon slices*
(chopped)	*watercress*

1. Soften the butter. Work in the lemon juice and chopped parsley. Add a little salt and pepper.
2. Spread the gills of the mushrooms with the seasoned butter.
3. Oil the grill pan and put the mushrooms into the pan.
4. Place the grid in the grill pan with the lamb chops on top.
5. Grill the meat until tender in which time the mushrooms should also be tender.

6. Put the meat onto a hot dish and carefully arrange the mushrooms on top.

7. Garnish the dish with lemon and watercress.

Poppins Pork

For 4

4 slices lean pork (6–8 oz each)	*½ teaspoon mustard*
1 oz butter	*1 apple*
2 tablespoons tomato purée	*1 leek*
½ pint stock	*½ lb open mushrooms*
¼ teaspoon ground ginger	*parsley (chopped)*

1. Heat the butter in a flameproof dish or shallow pan and seal the pork on both sides.

2. Blend tomato purée with stock, stir in ginger and mustard, pour over the meat.

3. Peel, core and slice the apple; cut leek into rings; quarter mushrooms. Arrange all these round the meat and sprinkle well with salt and pepper.

4. Cover with sheet of foil or lid and allow contents to simmer slowly for 40 minutes.

5. Remove cover, sprinkle with chopped parsley.

Somerset Chops

For 4

4 pork chops	*¼ pint dry cider*
1 oz butter	*¼ pint light stock*
1 tablespoon oil	*1 teaspoon mustard*
1 onion (chopped)	*1 tablespoon gherkins*
6 oz mushrooms (sliced)	*(sliced)*
1 oz flour	*watercress*

1. Grill the chops until tender; this will take about 20 minutes.
2. Heat the butter and oil in a pan and fry the onion and mushrooms until tender and lightly browned.
3. Stir in the flour and then add the cider and stock. Bring to the boil.
4. Add the mustard and gherkins and simmer for 2–3 minutes.
5. Put the chops onto a hot dish, pour over the sauce. Garnish with watercress.

Mushrooms Madeleine

For 4

6 oz liver
½ lb pie veal
6 oz streaky bacon

8 large cup mushrooms
½ teaspoon sage
¼ pint dry white wine

1. Mince the meats and stalks from the mushrooms together Stir in the crushed garlic. Season with salt, pepper and sage.
2. Pour in the wine, mix well and leave to stand for 2 hours.
3. Put the mushrooms into a shallow buttered ovenproof dish.
4. Fill the mushrooms with meat.
5. Cover the dish and bake in oven 350 degrees F, mark 4 for 40 minutes. Remove the lid for the last 10 minutes of cooking time.

Blanquette of Veal

For 4

1½ lb veal (breast or leg)
1 oz butter
1 tablespoon oil
2 large onions
4 cloves
4 oz carrots (thinly sliced)
1 stick celery (chopped)
bouquet garni

1–1¼ pints stock
1 oz butter with 1 oz flour
2 egg yolks
1 tablespoon lemon juice
nutmeg
parsley (chopped)
½ lb mushrooms (sliced)

1. Cut the veal into cubes. Heat the butter and oil in a large pan and turn the meat in hot fat until lightly browned.
2. Halve the onions; stick each half with a clove and put into the pan.
3. Add the carrots, celery and bouquet garni. Pour in the stock so that it just covers the ingredients.
4. Bring the contents to the boil; cover the pan with a lid and let simmer until the meat is tender.
5. Strain the stock into another pan and stir in the butter and flour blended together. Bring to the boil and simmer for 3 minutes.
6. Remove from the heat and stir in the egg yolks, beating well after each addition.
7. Add the lemon juice, a little nutmeg and parsley. Taste for seasoning.
8. Turn the mushrooms in a little hot oil in another pan. Season with salt and pepper and cook for 3 minutes.
9. Stir the meat and mushrooms into the sauce. Heat gently so that the dish is really hot without actually boiling.
10 Turn into a hot serving dish. Sprinkle with a little chopped parsley.

Jellied Meat Ring

For 6–8

2 packets aspic jelly powder
4 oz tin sweet red peppers
3 oz button mushrooms
1 tablespoon green pepper
(chopped)
1 tablespoon celery (chopped)

6 oz lean meat
(chicken, veal or pork—
diced, cooked)
1 tablespoon sherry
1 tablespoon lemon juice

1. Prepare 1 pint aspic jelly and leave aside to cool.
2. Drain and chop the red peppers. Slice 3–4 small mushrooms.
3. Chop the remaining mushrooms and mix with green pepper,

celery and meat. Season with salt and pepper and stir in sherry and lemon juice.

4. When the jelly is just beginning to set, pour a little of the jelly into a 7-inch ring mould and chill until set.

5. Set the sliced mushrooms in the mould; cover with aspic jelly and set.

6. Mix the red pepper with some jelly and turn into the mould. Leave to set.

7. Pour a layer of jelly only into the mould and set this.

8. Finally, mix the chopped meat mixture with the rest of the jelly and turn into the ring. Press down with the back of a spoon.

9. Chill until well set.

10. Dip the mould into a bowl of hot water, turn onto a plate. Serve with fresh salad.

Ham Horns

For 4

12 oz puff pastry
beaten egg
1 oz butter
4 oz mushrooms (chopped)
1 teaspoon lemon juice

4 oz ham (chopped)
1 tablespoon parsley
 (chopped)
½ pint coating cheese sauce

1. Roll out the pastry. Cut into strips and wind round the horn cases. Brush with beaten egg. Bake in oven 400 degrees F, mark 6 until crisp.

2. Heat the butter in a pan, add the mushrooms, season with salt and lemon juice. Cook until liquid has evaporated.

3. Stir mushrooms, ham and parsley into the cheese sauce.

4. Serve hot, filling the freshly baked pastry cases with the hot mixture.

Alternatively, allow the pastry cases to become cold; cool and chill the filling mixture. Fill the cases when ready to serve.

Tongue and Mushroom Mousse

For 4–6

    4 oz mushrooms   *1 tablespoon lemon juice*
    2 oz onion (sliced)   *1 tablespoon parsley*
    ½ pint beef stock   *(chopped)*
    ½ oz gelatin   *¼ pint double cream*
    ¾ lb cooked tongue   *½ teaspoon mustard*
    black pepper

1. Put the mushrooms and onion into a pan and pour in the stock. Simmer until tender.
2. Strain the stock and allow the vegetables to cool.
3. Dissolve the gelatin in the stock then put aside to cool.
4. Mince the mushrooms, onion and tongue.
5. Season this mixture with salt, freshly ground black pepper, lemon juice and parsley.
6. Whip the cream with the mustard.
7. Mix the tongue and mushroom mixture with the cream. Stir in the jelly when it is just about to set.
8. Turn into a mould and chill until set. Turn out onto a dish and serve with fresh salad.

Egg Duxelles

For 4

    1 lb mushrooms   *1 tablespoon parsley*
    2 oz butter   *(chopped)*
    4 oz onion (chopped)   *4 eggs*
    ¼ teaspoon mixed herbs   *½ pint coating cheese sauce*
    paprika   *1 slice white bread (toasted)*
    1 tablespoon lemon juice

1. Put aside 4–8 mushrooms to fry for garnish; chop the rest.
2. Heat butter in a large shallow pan, put in chopped mushrooms and onion. Season with herbs, salt, paprika and lemon juice. Simmer for about 10 minutes until all the liquid has evaporated; Stir in the parsley.

3. Hard boil the eggs, shell and keep warm in hot water.
4. Cover the base of four individual dishes with mushroom duxelles. Place an egg in each and coat with cheese sauce.
5. Garnish each dish with a triangle of toast and fried mushrooms.

Swiss Custard

For 4

1 clove garlic
2½ oz butter
6 slices white bread
10 oz mushrooms
6 oz Gruyère cheese (grated)
3 standard eggs

¼ pint dry white wine
¼ pint chicken stock
½ teaspoon mustard
Worcestershire sauce
black pepper

1. Crush the garlic finely. Blend thoroughly with the butter and spread on the bread.
2. Line an ovenproof dish with slices of bread with the buttered side out.
3. Slice the mushrooms, mix with the Gruyère cheese and put into the dish.
4. Beat the eggs with the wine and stock. Add the mustard and a few drops of Worcestershire sauce. Season with salt and ground black pepper. Pour over the mushrooms.
5. Bake in oven 350 degrees F, mark 4 for about 45 minutes.

Mushroom Quiche Lorraine

For 6

10 oz flaky pastry
1 oz butter
4 oz bacon rashers (cut in strips)
4 oz mushrooms (sliced)
4 oz Gruyère cheese

3 eggs
1 level tablespoon flour
¼ pint cream
⅓ pint milk
1 tablespoon butter (melted)

1. Line a 10-inch flan ring with the pastry.
2. Heat the butter in a pan and lightly fry the bacon and mushrooms.
3. Turn the bacon and mushrooms into the pastry case.
4. Cut the cheese into thin slices and arrange in the flan case.
5. Beat the eggs, flour, milk and cream together. Add 1 tablespoon melted butter, lightly browned; also salt and pepper.
6. Pour over the cheese and bake in oven 375 degrees F, mark 5 for about 35 minutes or until the custard is set and the top a golden brown.

Ravioli Niçoise

For 4

2 tablespoons olive oil	6 oz mushrooms (quartered)
1 large onion (roughly chopped)	salt and black pepper
	bouquet garni
3 courgettes (cubed)	1 tin ravioli with
1 large aubergine (cubed)	tomato sauce
4 tomatoes (skinned and quartered)	Parmesan cheese

1. Heat the olive oil in a large saucepan and sauté the onion until soft but not brown. Add courgettes and aubergines. Leave to cook, covered, until soft—about 30 minutes.
2. Stir in the tomatoes, mushrooms, seasoning and bouquet garni. Cover and simmer for 20 minutes. Remove pan lid and let liquid reduce for about 10 minutes over a moderate heat.
3. Heat ravioli as directed on the label.
4. Place the vegetables round the outside of a hot serving dish and pour the ravioli in the centre. Sprinkle with Parmesan cheese and brown under a hot grill.

Mushroom and Cheese Pizza

For 4

Dough:
6 oz self-raising flour   1¼ oz butter
½ teaspoon salt   about ¼ pint milk

Topping:
6 oz mushrooms   2 teaspoons mixed herbs
½ lb skinned tomatoes   3 oz Port Salut cheese
1 tablespoon spring onion   1 oz stuffed olives
    (chopped)   1 oz anchovy fillets
                                 3 tablespoons oil

1. Sieve flour and salt into a bowl, rub in the butter, bind with milk to make a soft dough.
2. Slice mushrooms, toss in hot oil, season with salt and cook for 2 minutes. Remove from the pan.
3. Put sliced tomatoes into the pan with onions and herbs; cook for 4 minutes.
4. Cool and drain off excess liquid.
5. Roll dough into a 10-inch circle spread with tomato mixture, top with mushrooms, sliced cheese, halved olives and anchovy fillets.
6. Bake in oven 400 degrees F, mark 6 for about 30 minutes.

Mushroom and Beer Puffs

For 6

8 oz flour   1 lb button mushrooms
2 eggs   deep fat for frying
½ pint beer   Tartare sauce

1. Put the flour and ½ teaspoon salt into a bowl. Break the eggs into the centre. Stir from the centre and gradually add the beer.
2. Beat with a wooden spoon or hand beater for 2–3 minutes. Leave to stand in a cool place.

3. Wash and dry the mushrooms. Turn in seasoned flour then coat in batter.
4. Fry in hot deep fat until golden and crisp. Drain on kitchen paper.
5. Serve piping hot with tartare sauce.

Champignons Flambé

For 4-8

1 lb button or cup mush-rooms	*1-2 teaspoons lemon juice*
2 oz butter	*2-3 tablespoons brandy*
1 teaspoon onion (grated)	*3 tablespoons double cream*
	parsley (chopped)

1. Keep the button mushrooms whole; cups will probably need slicing.
2. Heat the butter in a heavy pan, add the mushrooms and onion; sprinkle with lemon juice, salt and pepper.
3. Cook over a moderate heat for 3 minutes.
4. Pour in the brandy, set it alight and allow to burn until the flame goes out.
5. Pour in the cream, simmer gently for 2 minutes.
6. Turn into a hot serving dish and sprinkle with chopped parsley.

Swiss Fondue

For 6-8

¼ pint milk	*½ bottle dry white wine*
12 oz Gruyère cheese (sliced)	*2 oz butter*
1 clove garlic	*1 lb small button mush-rooms*

1. Pour the milk into a pan together with the sliced cheese. Cook gently over a low heat until the mixture begins to thicken.

2. Crush the garlic; put it into another pan with the wine and heat gently.
3. Pour the wine into the cheese pan and season with salt and pepper.
4. Cut the butter into small knobs and stir into the fondue.
5. Wash and dry the mushrooms. Cut into halves or quarters unless really small.
6. Using fondue forks, the guests dip the raw mushrooms into the hot fondue.

Cocktail Canapés

Small buttom mushrooms

Spreads: Pâté, cream cheese, scrambled egg, paste, butter or mayonnaise seasoned with anchovy, chives, smoked salmon, ham, crab, shrimp, garlic etc.

Garnishes: Chives, parsley, watercress, paprika, capers, gherkins, cucumber, nuts, olives, tomato, peppers etc.

1. Remove the stalks from the cleaned mushrooms. Put these aside for use in another dish.
2. Fill the mushrooms with a spread.
3. Top with a garnish.
4. Prepare the canapés, put them into a container with a lid, cover and keep cool in the refrigerator until ready to serve.

Party Dips

Allow 1 oz button mushrooms per person. Clean the mushrooms and cut into quarters. Using the stalk as a handle, the guest dips the mushroom quarters into a variety of sauces.

There are a number of bottled sauces on the market which are ideal or you may prefer to mix your own keeping them well chilled until ready to serve.

Caper Sauce

4 tablespoons mayonnaise
4 tablespoons cream
(whipped)
dash Worcestershire sauce

1 tablespoon capers
(chopped)
nutmeg

Blend together the first four ingredients; sprinkle with a little nutmeg just before serving.

Tomato Cream Sauce

¼ pint double cream
4 tablespoons tomato ketchup
2 tablespoons mayonnaise

½ teaspoon Worcestershire
sauce
garlic salt

Blend all the ingredients together adding garlic salt to taste.

Avocado Blues

1 avocado pear
2 oz blue cheese

celery salt

Mash the cheese and mix with the flesh from the pear. Beat until the mixture is creamy. Season with celery salt and add a few drops of milk if the mixture is too stiff.

Cucumber Cheese

½ cucumber
4 oz cream cheese

1 teaspoon onion (grated)
paprika

Grate the cucumber, sprinkle with salt and leave to stand for the water to drain out. Blend all the ingredients together, adding paprika to taste and as a garnish.

Crab Sour

3 oz crabmeat (or crab   *1 teaspoon chives (finely*
*   paste)*   *   chopped)*
4 oz soured cream

Blend the crab and cream together, season with salt and pepper. Scatter the chives over the top of the sauce.

Freezer Dishes

A SELECTION of dishes suitable for freezing for use at a later date. These dishes can also be stored in the domestic refrigerator for a day or two before use.

Multiply the recipes, so preparing a large quantity at a time, saving money and effort.

Vary the size of packs to suit your requirements, making packs for 1, 2, 4 or 6 portions. Pack in foil, foil trays, plastic bags, waxed cartons etc. If you use an ovenproof dish to freeze an oven-cooked dish, you can slip the frozen food out of the dish into foil, leaving the dish free for everyday use. Return the frozen food to the dish for cooking.

Mushroom Duxelles

2½ lb mushrooms
1 medium onion
2 oz butter

2 tablespoons parsley
(chopped)
black pepper

1. Mince the mushrooms and onion together.
2. Heat the butter in a large shallow pan. Add mushrooms, onion and parsley. Season with salt and freshly ground black pepper.
3. Cook over a moderate heat until all the liquid has evaporated.
4. Allow the mixture to become cold. Pack into cartons or sheets of foil, seal and freeze.
5. **To serve:** defrost at room temperature. Use as stuffing with breadcrumbs and herbs. Use as spread for toast, as a seasoning

for stews, casseroles and pies. Use to flavour soups, sauces and gravies.

Sautéed Mushrooms

2½ oz butter   1 teaspoon lemon juice
1 lb mushrooms (sliced)

1. Heat the butter in a shallow pan.
2. Add the mushrooms, season with salt, pepper and lemon juice; fry briskly until any liquid has evaporated and the mushrooms are lightly browned.
3. Allow mixture to become cold. Pack it in cartons or sheets of foil, seal and freeze.
4. **To serve:** defrost or use from frozen for any recipe calling for sautéed mushrooms. Ideal for omelettes and sauces.

Lemon and Mushroom Soup

For 5–6

2 oz butter   2 tablespoons parsley
1½ oz flour   (chopped)
1 pint chicken stock   juice of 1 lemon
½ pint milk   ¼ pint double cream
½ lb mushrooms (minced)

1. Heat the butter in a pan, stir in the flour and cook for a few moments.
2. Stir in the stock and bring to the boil.
3. Add milk, mushrooms and parsley. Season with salt, pepper and lemon juice to taste. Cook for 5 minutes.
4. Stir in the cream and allow to cool.
5. Turn into a dish of foil tray, cover and freeze.
6. **To serve:** heat very gently in a saucepan or put into an ovenproof dish, cover and heat in oven.

7. Sprinkle a little chopped parsley on the top just before serving.

Handsome Halibut

For 4

1¼ lb halibut	*2 hard-boiled eggs*
¾ pint fish stock	*1½ oz butter*
1 bay leaf	*1 oz flour*
1 lb mushrooms (minced)	*3 tablespoons double cream*
1 small onion (minced)	*2 egg yolks*
2 tablespoons parsley	*paprika*
(chopped)	

1. Cut the fish into 4 portions. Put it into an ovenproof dish. Pour in the fish stock. Season with salt, pepper and bay leaf. Cover and cook in oven 375 degrees F, mark 5 for about 30 minutes or until tender.
2. Put the mushrooms, onion and parsley into a pan. Sprinkle with salt and pepper and heat gently. Cook until all the liquid has evaporated.
3. Put mushroom mixture into the bottom of an ovenproof or foil dish.
4. Strain the fish and put the fish on top of the mushrooms.
5. Arrange the hard-boiled eggs, quartered, round the fish.
6. Melt the butter in a pan, stir in the flour and then the fish stock. Bring to the boil.
7. Season well. Remove from the heat and stir in cream and egg yolks. Heat gently then allow to cool.
8. Pour sauce over the fish. Make a pattern with a little paprika on the top of the dish.
9. When cold, cover and freeze.
10. **To serve:** Take dish from the freezer 45 minutes before cooking. Leave covered and cook in oven 350 degrees F, mark 4 for about 40 minutes.

Herring Fillets in Tomato Sauce

For 4–8

8 herring fillets   *2 shallots (sliced)*
juice of 1 large lemon   *½ pint tomato purée*
3 tablespoons olive oil   *Tarragon*
6 oz mushrooms (sliced)

1. Sprinkle the herring fillets with a little lemon juice and salt.
2. Heat the oil in a frying pan. Cook the fish for 1 minute each side.
3. Remove fish from the pan. Put mushrooms and shallots into the pan and cook for 3 minutes. Season with salt and freshly ground black pepper.
4. Pour in the rest of the lemon juice and the tomato purée. Add a pinch of Tarragon. Cook over a fierce heat for 3 minutes.
5. Reduce heat, return fish to the pan, cover with a lid or foil and simmer very slowly for 10 minutes.
6. Cool. Pack into foil trays or plastic bags. Freeze.
7. **To serve:** defrost at room temperature. Serve as cold or hot hors d'oeuvre. Also suitable as a main dish.

Individual Anchovy Pies

For 4

1½ lb white fish   *¾ oz flour*
½ pint milk   *1 tablespoon anchovy fillets*
2 oz butter   *(chopped)*
2 teaspoons onion (grated)   *1¼ lb creamed potatoes*
6 oz mushrooms (sliced)   *8 whole anchovy fillets*

1. Put the white fish into a pan. Season with salt and pepper. Pour over the milk and cook fish until is flakes easily.
2. Strain off the milk and keep for the sauce.

3. Flake the fish, removing any bones and skin.
4. Heat the butter in a pan, add onion and mushrooms and cook for 3 minutes.
5. Stir in the flour and then the strained milk. Bring to the boil and season with a little salt and pepper.
6. Fold the flaked fish and chopped anchovies into the sauce.
7. Turn into individual ovenproof dishes.
8. Top with creamed potatoes.
9. Make a pattern with the anchovy fillets on the potato, pressing them down into the potato.
10. Cover each dish and freeze.
11. When frozen, slide contents of each dish onto a sheet of foil; wrap closely and store in freezer.
12. **To serve:** return pies to the dishes; cook in oven 425 degrees F, mark 7 until top is lightly browned.

Scallops Macon Style

For 4

4 large scallops	3 oz butter
2 shallots (sliced)	1 tablespoon olive oil
4 oz button mushrooms (sliced)	1 small clove garlic
1 bay leaf	1 tablespoon parsley (chopped)
black pepper	4 tablespoons dried bread-
⅓ pint white Macon wine	crumbs

1. Clean the scallops and cut into thin slices.
2. Put into a bowl with the shallots and mushrooms. Add a bay leaf and plenty of freshly ground black pepper.
3. Warm the wine and pour into the bowl. Leave to stand for 2 hours.
4. Heat 1 oz butter with the olive oil in a pan and add the scallops, shallots and mushrooms.
5. Put the wine into another pan, cook over a fierce heat until it has reduced by half.

6. Pour wine into the scallop pan and simmer for 3 minutes.
7. Turn into the scallop shells and allow to cool.
8. Melt the remaining butter in a pan, add crushed garlic, parsley and breadcrumbs. Mix well. Scatter this mixture over the surface of the shells.
9. Cover the shells with foil and freeze.
10. **To serve:** take shells from the freezer about 30 minutes before cooking. Remove covers. Put into oven 375 degrees F, mark 5 for about 30 minutes. Serve with fresh brown bread and butter.

Chicken Pancake Rolls

For 4

½ *pint pancake batter*
fat for frying
2 oz butter
6 oz mushrooms (sliced)
1 oz flour
¼ *pint stock*

⅛ *pint cream*
½ *teaspoon mustard*
1 tablespoon gherkins (chopped)
½ *lb cooked chicken (chopped)*

1. Fry 8 pancakes in a small frying pan.
2. Heat the butter in a pan, add the mushrooms, sprinkle with salt and cook for 3 minutes.
3. Stir in the flour. Gradually add the stock, bring to the boil, then blend in the cream.
4. Stir in the mustard and gherkins, then the chopped chicken.
5. Check seasoning and simmer for 3 minutes.
6. Allow mixture to cool. Spread the pancakes with the mixture. Roll-up the pancakes.
7. Wrap the pancake rolls in foil then freeze.
8. **To serve:** put pancake rolls into an ovenproof dish. Leave to stand at room temperature for 30 minutes. Pour over a sauce or tin of soup of your choice (chicken, celery, mushroom, etc.) and bake in oven 375 degrees F, mark 5 for about 45 minutes.
9. Garnish with chopped parsley.

Kidney and Mushroom Bake

For 4

6–8 lamb's kidneys
8 tomatoes
4 oz streaky bacon
½ lb mushrooms

3 tablespoons oil
½ teaspoon mixed herbs
1 teaspoon lemon juice
black pepper

1. Skin, halve and core the kidneys. Skin and halve the tomatoes. Cut bacon into strips. Slice the mushrooms.
2. Heat the oil in a pan. Add the kidneys and cook for about 3 minutes.
3. Put the bacon and mushrooms into the pan with the kidneys and cook for 2 minutes.
4. Add the tomatoes, mixed herbs and lemon juice. Season with salt and freshly ground black pepper.
5. Cover and simmer gently for 10 minutes.
6. Turn mixture into a dish or foil tray.
7. When cold, cover and freeze.
8. **To serve:** heat in oven 400 degrees F, mark 6 for about 45 minutes or until really hot.

Moussaka—Mushroom Style

For 4–6

3 aubergines
olive oil
1 medium onion (sliced)
6 oz mushrooms (sliced)
1 oz butter

1 lb cooked lamb (minced)
3 tablespoons stock
2 bay leaves
½ pint tomato sauce (tinned)

1. Slice the aubergines and fry in hot oil until lightly browned on both sides.
2. Fry the onion and mushrooms in hot butter until tender.
3. Mix the minced lamb and stock together. Season well.

4. Put half the aubergines into an ovenproof dish or foil tray.
5. Add half the mushrooms and onion.
6. Turn all the meat into the dish. Place the bay leaves in the meat.
7. Cover with mushrooms and onions then the rest of the aubergines.
8. Pour over the tomato sauce and cook in oven 375 degrees F, mark 5 for about 50 minutes.
9. Allow to cool. Cover and freeze.
10. **To serve:** remove the cover and leave at room temperature for 45 minutes.
11. Arrange 2–3 oz processed Gruyère cheese, thinly sliced, over the top of the dish. Sprinkle with paprika and bake in oven 350 degrees F, mark 4 for about 30 minutes.

Pork and Mushroom Hotpot

For 4–6

1 lb lean pork (diced)	*½ pint dry cider*
½ lb bacon (diced)	*¼ pint stock*
½ lb cup mushrooms	*1 lb potatoes (sliced)*
black pepper	*paprika*
½ teaspoon sage	*2 tablespoons butter (melted)*

1. Put the pork, bacon and mushrooms into a casserole. Season well with salt, pepper and sage.
2. Pour in the cider and stock.
3. Cover the dish with sliced potatoes brushed with melted butter. Season with salt and paprika.
4. Cook in oven 375 degrees F, mark 5 for 1¼ hours.
5. Allow to become cold. Cover and freeze.
6. When frozen slide contents from the dish and wrap tightly in foil.
7. **To serve:** return the hot pot to the ovenproof dish and heat in oven 400 degrees F, mark 6 for about 45 minutes or until really hot. Garnish with chopped parsley.

Rabbit and Tomato Casserole

For 4

1 rabbit	*½ lb mushrooms (sliced)*
seasoned flour	*1¼ lb tomatoes*
4 tablespoons oil	*¼ pint dry cider*
4 oz onion (sliced)	*1 bay leaf*
1 green pepper (sliced)	*½ teaspoon Tarragon*

1. Cut the rabbit into joints. Coat with seasoned flour. Turn in hot oil for a minute or two. Put into a casserole dish.
2. Turn the onion and pepper in oil. Put into the casserole.
3. Add the mushrooms to the dish.
4. Skin the tomatoes, remove the pips, chop the flesh.
5. Mix tomatoes with the cider and herbs; add salt and pepper and turn into the casserole.
6. Cover and cook in oven 325 degrees F, mark 3 for 2 hours.
7. Cool. Turn into a dish or foil tray, cover and freeze.
8. **To serve:** heat in oven 350 degrees F, mark 4 for about 50 minutes.

Casseroled Steak

For 6

1½ lb stewing steak	*½ lb mushrooms (quartered)*
6 oz kidney	*1 clove garlic (crushed)*
2½ oz seasoned flour	*¾ pint beef stock*
3 tablespoons oil	*¼ pint dry red wine*
2 oz butter	*2 bay leaves*
1 large onion (sliced)	

1. Cut the steak and kidney into cubes and turn in seasoned flour.
2. Heat butter and oil in a pan. Put the meat into the pan and cook until sealed on all sides. Turn meat into a casserole dish.

3. Put onion, mushrooms and garlic into the dish.
4. Stir the remaining seasoned flour into the pan juices; add the stock and wine. Season with salt, pepper and bay leaves. Bring to the boil.
5. Pour into the casserole, cover with the lid. Cook in oven 325 degrees F, mark 3 for 2½–3 hours.
6. Cool. Turn into a dish or foil tray, cover and freeze.
7. **To serve:** heat (from frozen) in oven 350 degrees F, mark 4 for about 50 minutes.

Alternatively, defrost the contents of the dish, turn into a pie-dish and top with puff pastry. Brush with beaten egg and bake in oven 425 degrees F, mark 7 for about 35 minutes.

Special Shepherd's Pie

For 4

¾ *lb cooked meat (minced)*	*1 oz butter*
¼ *pint gravy or sauce*	*1 tablespoon chives (chopped)*
½ *lb mushrooms (sliced)*	*1–1½ lb potatoes (creamed)*

1. Mix the minced meat with enough gravy to moisten the meat; season well with salt and pepper. Turn into an ovenproof dish or foil tray.
2. Turn the mushrooms in hot butter, add salt and pepper; cook over a fierce heat for 2 minutes. Sprinkle with chopped chives and turn into the dish.
3. Cover with creamed potato. Smooth and decorate. Cover with a lid or foil.
4. Freeze.
5. **To serve:** remove the cover. Dot with butter or brush with beaten egg. Bake in oven 425 degrees F, mark 7 for about 1 hour if cooked from frozen.

Veal and Mushroom Cream

For 4

1½ oz butter
4 oz minced bacon
1 small clove garlic
½ lb mushrooms (chopped)
1 lb minced veal

black pepper
1 tablespoon lemon juice
1 teaspoon flour
½ pint cream of mushroom
soup

1. Heat the butter in a pan, add the bacon and crushed garlic and cook for 1 minute.
2. Add the mushrooms and veal, season with salt, freshly ground black pepper and lemon juice. Stir over a moderate heat for about 4 minutes.
3. Sprinkle the flour into the pan and mix well.
4. Add the soup and simmer for 15 minutes, covering the pan with a well-fitting lid.
5. Cool the mixture. Turn into a foil tray or dish. Cover and freeze.
6. **To serve:** defrost at room temperature. Heat through in a saucepan. Turn into a hot dish and garnish with slices of lemon and sprigs of parsley.

Veal Valencia

For 4

1 lb pie veal
4 oz streaky bacon
½ lb mushrooms
1 onion
1 clove garlic
3 tablespoons oil
1 tablespoon flour

1 large tin tomatoes
⅛–¼ pint stock
2 oz cheese (grated)
2 tablespoons breadcrumbs
1 tablespoon parsley
(chopped)

1. Cut the veal into cubes. Chop the bacon. Quarter the mushrooms. Slice the onion and crush the garlic.

2. Heat the oil in a large pan and add the above ingredients. Turn over a moderate heat for about 4 minutes.

3. Sprinkle the flour into the pan and mix well.

4. Turn the tomatoes and stock into the pan. Season with salt and pepper and stir thoroughly.

5. Cover pan with a lid or foil and simmer very gently for about 1 hour.

6. Cool the mixture and put into a foil tray or dish. Scatter cheese, breadcrumbs and parsley over the top. Cover and freeze.

7. **To serve:** remove the cover, put dish into oven 400 degrees F, mark 6 for about 45 minutes or until really hot and brown on top.

Index

Savouries, Sardine, 35
  Smoked Salmon, 46
Scallops, 6
  in wine, 112
  Macon style, 137
Scotch Mushrooms, 77
Shrimp and Cucumber Salad, 94
Simon's Savoury, 32
Smoked Haddock and Mushroom
  Omelette, 33
Smoked Salmon Savouries, 46
Snacks, Bacon, 22
Soho Chicken, 116
Somerset Chops, 119
Soup,
  Cream of Mushroom, 53
  Fish with Mushrooms, 54
  Lemon and Mushroom, 134
Sour Crab, 130
Sour Cream Coleslaw, 95
Soya Mushroom Savoury, 20
Spanish Bake, 14
Special Burgundy, 97
  Shepherd's Pie, 142
Steak,
  Casseroled, 141
  Kidney and Mushroom Pie, 65
Steaks, Orange, 115
Stew, Beef, 64
Stuffed Loin of Pork, 68
  Mushrooms, 9
  Plaice Fillets, 110
Stuffing, Mushroom and Bacon, 70
Sunset Salad, 95
Supreme, Oxtail and Mushroom,
  65

Suzanne, Liver, 44
Sweetcorn, Frankfurter, 26
Sweet Salad with Chicken, 96
Swiss Custard, 124
  Fondue, 127

TARTARE SALAD, 94
Thousand Island Dreams, 43
Toast, Herring Roes on, 36
Tomato Cream Sauce, 129
Tomato Fish Tumble, 61
Tongue and Mushroom Mousse,
  123
Trout, Green Collared, 109
Tumble, Tomato fish, 61
Tuna Bake, Creamed, 62

VALENCIA VEAL, 143
Veal and Mushroom Cream, 143
Veal,
  Blanquette of, 120
  Valencia, 143
  Vitesse, 49
Venetian Liver, 9
Vinaigrette, Mushroom and
  Almond, 92
Vitesse Veal, 49
Vol-au-vents, egg and mushroom,
  30

WELSH RAREBIT WITH MUSHROOM,
  34
Wheel, Frankfurter, 77
White Grape Cocktail, 42
Wine, Scallops in, 112